D0973368

Getting Along *almost* With Your
ADULT KIDS

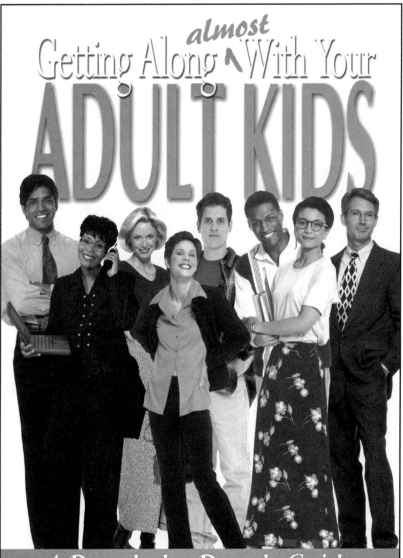

Getting Along ^almost With Your

ADULT KIDS

A Decade-by-Decade Guide

Lois Leiderman Davitz, Ph.D.
& Joel R. Davitz, Ph.D.

 SORIN BOOKS   Notre Dame, IN

© 2003 by Lois Leiderman Davitz and Joel R. Davitz

www.sorinbooks.com

International Standard Book Number: 1-893732-61-4

Cover and text design by Brian C. Conley

Printed and bound in the United States of America.

Library of Congress Cataloging-in-Publication Data
Davitz, Lois Jean.
    Getting along (almost) with your adult kids : a decade-by-decade guide
/ Lois Leiderman Davitz, Joel R. Davitz.
            p. cm.
        ISBN 1-893732-61-4
    1. Parent and adult child. I. Davitz, Joel Robert. II. Title.

HQ755.86.D38 2003
306.874--dc21

                                                    2003007146

CONTENTS

INTRODUCTION:
Happily Getting Along
With Your Adult Children

When people talk about parenting, they usually are referring to preschoolers, school-aged youngsters, or teenagers. This stems from the commonly held belief that the major tasks of parenting are finished when your child is no longer a teenager. In fact, parenting doesn't stop when your child reaches 20, it merely changes.

True enough, you are no longer the primary caretaker concerned with fulfilling your child's basic needs. And you are not the teacher, guide, or principal role model you were at an earlier time, responsible for helping your child acquire basic skills of everyday living as well as inculcating a sense of morality and a set of meaningful values. Those parenting tasks are, for the most part, a matter of the past.

Nevertheless, you inevitably remain a most significant person in your child's life, with new opportunities, new responsibilities, and new sources of happiness and fulfillment. It is this change in the nature of parenting an adult child that is the topic of this book.

A POINT OF VIEW

Before discussing specific issues of parenting an adult child, we would like to clarify our basic point of view with regard to parenting. This point of view has guided our discussion of various aspects of parental experience and has certainly influenced our recommendations for parental behavior.

We began with the recognition that almost all human relationships involve extrinsic goals. These are goals that go beyond the immediate relationship. For example, in a work situation, these goals might be making money or gaining power. In a social situation, these extrinsic goals might be gaining status or achieving a sense of belonging. In other words, when we relate to one another in daily life, there is the immediate, ongoing relationship, and there are also goals that extend beyond that immediate relationship.

These extrinsic goals are undoubtedly important in parenting a younger child. These are the long-term, child-rearing goals that all parents have in relating to their children. A parent who is teaching a child everyday manners also aims to instill in the child a sense of social sensitivity and concern for others that goes far beyond the immediate parent-child interaction. Similarly, after an adolescent has repeatedly transgressed some explicit limits, a parent might ground the teenager, sacrificing the pleasure of current cordial relations for the sake of the long-term goal of the adolescent learning about respecting limits and fulfilling responsibilities.

But there is a significant difference when it comes to parenting your adult child. In any particular instance, there may be some extrinsic goals of the sort we have mentioned, but in general, they are much less important than the immediate *intrinsic value of the relationship itself*. It's the relationship itself that is a parent's first and foremost concern. Our primary goal in relating to our adult children is not to make money, gain status, achieve power or prestige. And by and large, we are no longer concerned with taking care of basic needs or teaching the difference between right and wrong.

Our point of view—and it guides our choice of parenting behaviors—is the intrinsic value of the relationship with our adult child. This leads to a central criterion we use to evaluate our parenting behaviors: *Does our behavior foster and reinforce a loving relationship with our child, or does it harm that loving relationship?*

As we have grown older, we have become increasingly convinced that this is far more important than trying to make sure our child does the "right" thing, gaining our child's attention or respect, or fulfilling our own needs and expectations in our role as parents.

A DEVELOPMENTAL FRAMEWORK

Parenting an adult child covers a wide range of problems over a relatively wide span of time. We therefore need a framework, a way of approaching these matters that will help us understand the changes and complexities that parents encounter. We have found that a developmental framework is most useful in this regard.

Our discussion of parenting, therefore, is organized in terms of decades of an adult child's life: 20–29, 30–39, 40–49, and 50-plus. For each decade, we briefly describe the typical developmental tasks of the decade and then consider the most common parenting issues of that period.

Although we find this developmental framework to be a useful tool in thinking about parenting adult children, we don't want you to take this framework as a set of hard and fast rules that are cast in stone. First of all, the division by decades, 20–29, 30–39, etc., is only approximate. While there are indeed distinct developmental tasks generally associated with each decade, it would be absurd to assume that these developmental tasks begin on the morning of a person's twentieth birthday and are completed at the end of the person's twenty-ninth year.

Much more important than the specific timing involved is understanding that an adult child changes and develops over time and that parenting must also appropriately change and develop over time. Second, we must recognize that there are wide individual differences in all matters considered in this volume. A 50-year-old may be behaving like a typical 20-year-old while a 30-year-old may be going through the psychologically fidgety time more commonly associated with the early 40s. Such individual differences are simply a fact of life that all of us must accept. Therefore, recognizing that these individual differences undoubtedly exist, we have organized our discussion of parenting on the basis of common trends and generally shared experiences.

THE TERRIBLE TWENTIES
Parenting the Adult Child From 20–29

THE BEGINNING OF AN ERA

With a catch in your throat you think to yourself, "Wasn't it just yesterday that my 20-year-old was a teenager? Do I shut the door to the bedroom, leave everything in place for the unlikely day when my child might return? Do I give a battered desk away, take down a bulletin board marked with all sorts of dates: proms, graduation, recitals, back-to-school nights, athletic events, school vacations? Should I turn the room into a TV hideaway?

"People talk about empty nest shock and the adjustments that have to be made when kids leave home. Have I, too, reached that stage in life? Nineteen years and my parenting days are over? It's no wonder I feel wistful."

We urge you to forget such sentimental thoughts. Parents mistakenly believe their parenting days are finished when a child turns 20. That is far from the case. There is no need for nostalgia. Parenting never ends. What changes are the demands, and most important, your behavior in relationship to your adult kids.

The nineteen years of parenting you've just experienced have little to do with what is in store after your kids turn 20. Compared to the excitement and diversity of the next decades, parenting from 0 to 19 will seem like a piece of cake. Therefore, relax, sit down in a comfortable chair, and enjoy a favorite drink and snacks while we do our best to prepare you for the excitement of discovering how to relate to adult children. We're confident the reward for your efforts will be a happy, productive, fulfilling, and exciting relationship. This is a goal worth achieving.

MAJOR DEVELOPMENTAL TASKS

The major developmental task of 20- to 29-year-olds is to establish their identity in the world of adults. In other words, 20s must face and answer the question, "Who am I as an adult?"

"Look Mom, I'm not a kid anymore. Stop treating me like one." Twenty-year-olds strut with a new confidence. In their eyes, they're no longer children. Just a short time ago they were teenagers. Adults didn't always treat them with the respect they deserved. Teenage behavior was watched over, scrutinized, commented upon, and in many ways controlled by parental authority. Well, that phase of life has ended. When you're 20, it's a different story. Twenty is an adult, at least in the 20-year-old's mind.

It's time to put photos of childish behavior away in a shoebox to be stored in the basement along with other teenage mementos. Everything is different—well, almost different. Clothes and hairstyles radically change; a stud in the pierced nose may be removed. Distinctive signs of teen years—blasting car stereos, giggles, wild laughter, moody withdrawals, slamming doors, sullen looks—fade away one by one. It's not that they are gone forever. Bits and pieces of the behavior will reappear in various forms and in varying degrees later on in life. Right now, however, a lot of the abandon and ebullience that characterized the teens goes underground.

Although 20s are eager to grow up, they haven't the slightest intention of becoming settled oldsters. The image of settling down behind a picket fence in a house with window boxes is dreaded. When 20s think of lifestyles that appeal to them, far more dramatic images come to mind. There's a hint of the 40s mentality in their desire to break loose from traditional paths.

However, right now 20s haven't had a lot of experience being adults. They can't honestly come up with a blueprint of the kind of destiny they see for themselves. But then specifics aren't as important, just as long as the 20s are doing something that represents a break with the past. Old high school buddies often get lost somewhere along the way in growing up. New friendships develop. Parents may not know the names, much less get a chance to meet these people.

Home may still be a refuge. Most of the time it's a brief stopping-off place on vacations during a college break. For working 20s, the parental home has value as a temporary base until other arrangements can be made. And for still others, home is a convenient place to do laundry.

"I see my 22-year-old daughter once a week. She likes doing her laundry in our basement. The building where she lives doesn't have a laundry room. She hates launderettes. I find it infuriating that much of our relationship is a quick conversation about detergent. She had the nerve to complain the other day because I ran out of her favorite cold water wash."

It's not that the 20s are out to abandon their parents. What really concerns them, however, is their own identity. Most important, they want to make very sure this identity is not only separate but a lot different from their parents'. Moms and dads, by definition, are old-fashioned, even if this is far from reality. Parents who aren't happy about being viewed in this way have to be patient. In a few decades their kids will sort out the distortions and come to the conclusion that their parents are not really stodgy and unreasonable as they once thought. In fact, many 20s kids who rejected their parents' values eventually refer to their parents as good role models. They may further shock their parents by quoting them. It is difficult for parents to imagine such an about-face on the part of their kids. You might have to wait until your children are in their 50s, but we assure you it will eventually happen.

At the moment, trying to relate to 20s who at times are totally caught up in their own egos is often an overwhelming challenge. Twenties kids have tunnel vision. They can't see much of the world outside of their own lives. However, this is exactly how it should be. Think of the 20s from their perspective. They've emerged from the restraining teen years. Currently all their energies are devoted to self-discovery, where they are headed in life. What makes parents happy is the furthest thought from their minds. If anything, it's time to escape from moms and dads looking over their shoulders.

Escaping from parents, sometimes both psychologically and physically, in no way implies that young 20s are out to sever family bonds. Who else but mom or dad can come up with a much needed deposit on a fantastic one-bedroom apartment to be shared with four buddies! There's a lot of unused furniture at home that is begging for a place to be stored. And best of all, there's a filled refrigerator a young 20s is welcome to search for snacks. Twenties stay in contact in this transition period even if visits are short, sometimes widely spaced apart, and cell phone calls are made on the run.

This striving for independence, which necessarily involves pushing parents away, is a crucial developmental stage. In the teens, parents have served as sounding boards, handing out advice—wanted or not wanted. Teens half-listened. But in the 20s it's preferable not to turn to the parents for help with problems. Peers are far better consultants. Peers know what romantic agony means. Peers understand and can empathize when a job goes sour or decisions about careers or college courses must be made.

Later in life, when these same 20s are decades older and more secure, parents will have a chance to express their opinions. The shock will come when their advice is actually sought out! In the 20s, however, the important thing is to struggle by oneself, consulting with friends the same age to find answers to the big questions of life. And these questions can be overwhelming.

Most 20s have not done a lot of introspection. No wonder they may look back longingly on their teen years. Life was carefree. Major decisions mostly involved whether to hang out at the mall, join the debate or glee club, whom to ask to the prom, what to wear. Sure, there were parental intrusions, annoyances about curfews, and spending too much of the parents' money, arguments with best friends, peer pressures, but life's BIG questions rarely entered their consciousness.

In contrast, 20s think about: "What am I going to do with my life? What is my future? I think I deserve a break, going off for six months to find myself. Do I want a relationship with a significant other? If I live with someone, does this mean I have to marry that person? I'm not ready for marriage. In fact, I'm not so sure I ever want to get married. Well, maybe someday. Meanwhile I want to do so many things. My parents expect a great deal from me. I can't take their demands. They don't understand I don't want to settle down and be like them, living in a split-level house on a tree-shaded street."

Now that the teen has turned 20, a whole brave new world beckons. To be young and twenty with a glint in one's eye, a spring in one's step, ready for adventure and the excitement of living as an adult, is a wonderful thing. Perhaps six months trekking in the Himalayas is not such a bad idea. Maybe just as good would be the purchase of a motorcycle and a cross-country adventure.

There are a lot of things 20s have to sort out about themselves. There's tension, but that makes sense. Having just taken a giant step from the shelter of the teen years onto the ladder of adulthood, their footing is far from secure. In fact, it's downright shaky. In their favor, however, is the buoyancy of youth, the belief in being invulnerable, and the prospect of endless tomorrows.

It's important that young 20s remain blissfully unaware that they will once again be facing these troublesome questions in their 40s. Right now they deserve to enjoy their euphoria, viewing the world as Calaban did in *A Midsummer Night's Dream* when he cried out, "Oh brave new world." For the teen turned 20, it is a brave new world to be discovered and experienced to the fullest.

"DEEP DOWN, I'D LIKE MY KID SETTLED"

"Didn't you major in history in college and plan on being a teacher?"

"I thought you said you wanted to be a zoologist? That's why you took biology."

"Don't you want to start working in your uncle's cleaning business? He's offered you a great job. The store will be yours someday."

"Didn't you once say you like business? Have you thought about becoming a CPA?"

Twenties kids often face an onslaught of questioning about career goals from their parents.

"My daughter told me to stop treating her like she's 16. She's 23. Well, I'd like to tell her if she's so concerned about being treated like an adult, she should act like one. I guess what bothers me is after four years of college, all she does is mope around the house complaining she doesn't know what she wants to do with her life. One day she's going to be an actress, the next a dancer. All this is said in between telling me she thinks she'll become a writer. It's impossible to get her to sit down and talk seriously."

Having survived the ups and downs and the mood swings of the teenage years, parents may long for relief, peace, and quiet. They may not fully share, much less appreciate, the 20s' unsettled feelings. No wonder there are conflicts between parents and their kids. Deep down each of them views life through a different lens.

Mistakenly, parents of 20- to 29-year-olds expect their children to be adults as *parents* define adulthood. This implicitly means a sense of purpose and direction in life best represented by a meaningful career. The confusion 20s experience about their future frequently makes parents edgy. Subtly and not so subtly parents may try to push their kids toward goals kids couldn't care less about pursuing.

Parents forget that early 20s children face a reality shock. For example, if they lived away at college, their daily activities escaped parental scrutiny. Suddenly kids feel under microscopic observation. No wonder many long for escape. If the kids live in New York, they may fantasize about California. If they live in California, they may idealize the East Coast. And if they're located somewhere in middle America, dreams will range all over the fifty states.

Parents, on the other hand, operate with a different agenda in mind. They're adept at coming up with challenging comments such as one father made to his son, "When I was your age, I knew exactly what I was going to do with my life. I didn't have help from parents to pay for my education. I worked. It took me five years to graduate."

Later the father told us privately, "In this country, we don't make enough demands on kids. They can take as long as they want to grow up. I blame parents. I blame my wife. I can't believe her sometimes. She can worry about everything—including whether a 24-year-old son is keeping his feet dry with warm socks in winter."

We shall withhold judgment. On the one hand, we sympathize with the father. He's just paid dearly for three children to go to college. The 24-year-old has been out of school for nearly two years and is still trying to find himself. The father feels he deserves a break from decades of parenting. "My son lives at home. If you listened to him, he thinks there are whole string of tomorrows out there. He has no idea about making life decisions for himself."

We also understand the son. Why should he settle down into a groove? The steady routine of his father's life, going to work every morning, returning at 7:00 every evening, strikes him as a deadly way to live. Shouldn't life always be an exciting adventure? Is it necessary to pursue one career, stay with the same company rather than have the excitement of change? Also, what is so wrong with falling in and out of love monthly? The differences in attitudes, goals, and desires between 20s and their parents frequently cause rifts. With understanding on the part of parents, clashes between the two could be prevented or at least markedly reduced. There is a reason that 20s kids can't be expected to understand what is going on. They're far too immersed in their personal lives. It's not all that easy to step out of their own psyches and look at themselves objectively. Why should they? If the parents want to sit and stew about their kids' lives, well, that's their problem.

THE SELECTIVE MEMORIES OF PARENTS

Given the very normal unrest of the early 20s, it's not the time for parents to bring up rapturous stories of their own remarkable youth when they knowingly and confidently pursued a goal. When one is giving a moral lecture or a pep talk, particularly to one's own kids, there's a great temptation to present ourselves in the best possible light.

The most effective way to handle 20s kids in this kind of situation is to withhold lectures, judgmental comments, and unwanted advice. Twenties kids, and in fact kids of all ages, would be a lot happier not having to sit and listen to a well-rehearsed, familiar stock of parental memories. Just between us, this won't be the first time your adult child is going to feel unsettled.

What kids need most at this stage in life is a little breathing space, time to sort matters out in their own minds. When that first dream job they apply for doesn't work out or the big love of their life ends in heartbreak, there's no need for parents to jump in with their reasoned evaluation of what happened.

Above all, avoid comparisons with other children. "If I listened to my mother and believed her," one 25-year-old woman told us, "everyone my age is engaged to a dream come true, has a super job, and the families are planning wonderful weddings. That's not the way my life is going. I asked my mom,

'Do you have a problem? Do you feel stuck with me as a daughter?' She got so hurt. She said that's not what she meant at all. 'Really,' I asked her, 'What *did* you mean?'"

The last thing kids need at any age is parental pressure. "What are you going to do with the rest of your life?" When you're 20 and starting out, life down the road is about the last thing in the world you're thinking about. You aren't even sure you ever want to think about the future. I vividly recall being interviewed for a dream position when I was 23 years old. The "old" man (from my perspective at the time) who interviewed me said at the conclusion of our meeting, "Now I want to tell you about the retirement plan we have." He proceeded to describe all the benefits I would be eligible for forty-two years later. The subject was meaningful for him. I fled from the office shaken.

Twenties don't want to hear about pensions, nor do they want to hear wonderful stories about relatives or neighbors' children their age who are all focused and pursuing professional goals in a neat, orderly fashion.

What can parents offer instead that will make all the difference? The answer is quite simple: the comfort of your presence, your being there to ease the shock of any setback. *The fewer words said the better!* Remind yourself that you survived. They will, too! It's comforting to know that most people do eventually grow up!

DON'T LOSE YOUR COOL

When a 20- to 29-year-old doesn't follow a conventional pattern or lacks direction and focus, parents become edgy. "He left his job. He has a college degree. He's 27 and tells me he is going to be a folk singer and take guitar lessons. He hasn't sung since junior high school. This doesn't make sense. My son has so many other gifts."

We certainly agree that this kind of announcement from a fair-haired boy is tough for a parent to accept. Becoming a folk singer seems an unlikely ambition for a 27-year-old. How old were the Beatles when they began? How old was Elvis? Has my son lost his sanity? Parents are justifiably bewildered. It's at critical times like this that an extra measure of patience is needed for a parent to survive.

Time will take care of a lot of problems. The challenge is for parents to wait out the low periods. The 20s decade is filled with tough moments that seem like hurdles never to be jumped. If you can wait and not get exhausted in the waiting process, you will be better prepared to cope with the ups and downs of the next decades with your kids.

We remember, even though it was many years ago, a long walk with our son who was in his early 20s. We listened, open-mouthed—stunned is a more appropriate word—when he confided that he was thinking of becoming a standup comic. He does have a fantastic sense of humor. We can't resist telling you how enchanting he was as a clown in a third-grade performance. That show is not forgotten. We have the photos in case you're interested. Unfortunately, his current 20- to 29-year-old friends also recognized his talent. Several suggested he do monologues professionally.

Being a standup comic sounded intriguing. What had happened to his education as a mathematical statistician? He had a job in this field. We thought he was planning to go on to graduate school to finish his doctorate.

Choking, we mumbled in strained voices, "How would you get started in this kind of career?" As psychologists we didn't want to put a damper on our son's ambition. Always be encouraging. That's the professional attitude to take.

Well, he thought, he might get a job in a local cocktail lounge as a performer. Our hearts rapidly palpitating, blood pressure skyrocketing, terrorized we listened to the plan. We aren't snobs. There's nothing inherently wrong with being a comedian. Jerry Seinfeld has made millions. Was it possible our son, too, could become a millionaire telling jokes? Depressed, we listened to a description of this ambition that seemed to be coming at the wrong age, the wrong timing—truly out of the blue.

As parents there wasn't much we could do. If he were a teenager we could do some talking, lecturing, come up with full-blown guidance of some sort. We could even have threatened cutting off financial support.

However, he was working. We weren't providing money for his living. The troubling part for parents of 20- to 29-year-olds is when something isn't going according to their expectations they can't collar their child, sit them down for a chat, and then cut off an allowance when the behavior doesn't fall into line.

Our opinions weren't wanted. We behaved in the only way possible—as silent, agonized, pained, unhappy onlookers. We tried to comfort ourselves by thinking, "This stage will pass." It took every ounce of self-control we could muster to conceal our stress. Luckily we were so shocked that we were speechless. We say luckily because we realized in a more rational moment that if we had expressed our real anxiety, and negative feelings, our onslaught of angry words would have been destructive to him and our relationship.

When children *below* 20 come up with what parents feel are harebrained schemes or behave in outlandish ways, parental hugs and long talk sessions usually can convince kids "to come around" and behave more sensibly. After 20, old-fashioned parental approaches don't work. Parents are forced into the role of observer.

It won't do any good to sweat and fume, especially not to the 20- to 29-year-old. Overreacting or focusing on minor issues, obsessing about them, will just make problems worse. Making emotional mountains out of trivial molehills will be the *most destructive thing* you can do for your own sanity and for the relationship between you and your child.

As a footnote to our story, when we asked this same son in his 40s if he had been serious that time about becoming a standup comic, he looked at us as if we had "lost it." *What was absurd was not his indulging in a youthful fantasy, but that he had made the mistake of sharing it with us. We had taken him seriously.*

We didn't tell him at the time about our own history. When we were about the same age as our son, we had flirted with various career options. Lois had thought of becoming an actress. A severe problem with stage fright thwarted pursuit of this career.

World War II had ended, and Joel was discharged from the Navy. As a way of earning some money he thought it might be possible to become a radio announcer. Everyone said he had a very nice speaking voice. He also was an avid reader. One audition ended this ambition. We assure you it was just an oversight on our part that we never told our son these stories until now.

A HEALTHY BIT OF INSENSITIVITY CAN GO A LONG WAY TOWARD SMOOTHING RELATIONSHIPS

We've spent our professional careers as psychologists, and in the past we have often emphasized the importance of being sensitive to other people's feelings. However, in the wisdom of our senior years, we've come to the conclusion that a little healthy insensitivity to your adult child's minor stresses will go a long way toward making your parenting life a lot easier.

Although this is the first time we're introducing the insensitivity mantra, we'll be coming back to it over and over again. "Nothing hurts more than when something bad happens to my 26-year-old daughter," one parent told us. Therefore, when a 20- to 29-year-old has problems, whether it be with a girlfriend, boyfriend, job, or life in general, parents are going to feel and react to the tension unless they practice a little distancing, insensitivity, and nonreacting.

Parents of 20s also have to be especially wary of falling into a vicious circle of hostility and counterhostility. They have to remind themselves that their 20s child wants to assume control of his or her life. Just out of teen dependency, they are busy striving for total independence. One foot may still be at home. They may even be living at home. Nonetheless, they're eager to stand on their own two feet.

When a parent of this age steps in, trying to give too much advice, trying to help too much, expect irritation and rejection. Then what happens? Well-intentioned advice and actions on your part are resented. You feel hurt and angry. You become more insistent, maybe a bit hostile. The level of hostility escalates and before you know it you and your child are enraged at each other.

"I've had enough of you parents in my life."

And then your retort. "How can you talk to me that way after all I've done for you? Who do you think loaned you the money for your car. . . ?"

"I intend to pay everything back."

"I didn't ask for the money. I was just trying to help you understand."

"Understand what? That you still want to run my life? I'm not a kid any longer."

It's only the rare parent who at one time or another hasn't had some variation of the verbal exchange we've just noted. Volatile exchanges that occur between adult children and parents run the risk of incurring hard feelings and resentment that may last for years. Instead of falling into the trap of the vicious circle of hostility and counterhostility, try a little bit of insensitivity.

"I'M SORRY, LET'S MOVE ON"

What should parents do if hurt feelings and an undercurrent of anger remain after a quarrel? Who is responsible for being the first to say, "I'm sorry"? Who should be the first to bend or initiate reconciliation? In our interviews with parents, we encountered many who dug their heels in and wanted an apology, especially if they thought they were in the right.

"I don't care what my daughter says. I am her mother. She should have *respect* for me. I don't think she should ever forget this, and until she says, 'I'm sorry,' I wash my hands of her."

We met fathers who strongly and stubbornly concurred with this mother. For these individuals, being right or wrong is not the point. What really matters for them is whether the child shows respect for the parent. But is respect really the important issue? Or is the parental demand for an apology just a cover for the parent to make sure he or she still has authority?

After strong words and flowing adrenaline, it takes a great deal of strength to be the first to say, "Let's cool it!" We're not advocating that parents crawl, demean, or humble themselves. However, if an apology is warranted for what you contributed to the vicious circle of hostile interaction, recognize your contribution. *Be the one who first says, "I'm sorry."*

Not all parents will agree with our thinking. We believe parents have to forget who is right or who is wrong. *No argument is worth hurting the long-term relationship between you and your child.*

One mother we talked to complained because her son didn't stop to chat with her when he came home. "He walks in the house, goes right up to his room, and doesn't say a word. It bothers me because he'll drink all the sodas in the fridge and never tell us. If he only said something, I would buy more."

It doesn't take any fancy interpretation to understand that the mother couldn't have cared less about the sodas. What really bothered her was her son's rushing into the house, not chatting. The mother's feelings were hurt. "I finally told my son his behavior toward me was inexcusable. He owed me an apology."

Bitter words followed between the two. And, as is the case during an argument, lots of truths, half-truths, imagined slights, and real slights dredged up from the past became intertwined. Both of the antagonists built up the best defense possible for their behavior. It didn't take long for doors to slam, leaving hard feelings as a bitter aftermath. The mother and son still were not on speaking terms after a number of years.

An argument that began with cans of soda led to several years of hurt feelings. All of this might have been avoided if the mother had stopped for a moment, recognized how she had contributed to the vicious circle of hostile interactions, and said, "I'm sorry. Let's start over."

On a personal level we recall an incident with a parent when Joel and I were in our early 20s. We had purchased a pound of outrageously priced cookies. My mother-in-law was infuriated with the expenditure. She felt that since Joel and I were hardly affluent at the time, our wasting money on such an extravagance was indicative of our generally irresponsible attitude toward money, which frankly was the case.

Like most naive 20s, we had the innocent idea that the money one earns is to be spent as soon as it enters your pocket. Most important, the money should be spent in *pleasurable* ways. Of course, we would become wiser as we grew older. Thirties kids know better; 40s even more, and 50s still even more. All right-minded adults know the purpose of money is to be stashed away, hoarded, banked to earn interest, counted frequently, put in various accounts, and saved for college expenses, redoing an antiquated bathroom, finishing a basement, or retirement. It is quite inappropriate to take money you don't have a lot of and spend it on chocolate chip cookies with macadamia nuts. Just think of what that money would have earned if we had put it safely away in a bank for the last fifty years.

Not one person in the family escaped hearing about our extravagant indulgence. Shaking heads and derision were the reactions to what became known as the *chocolate chip cookie escapade*. The purchase triggered off irritation; however, the ensuing resentment was that we refused to apologize or show any regret for our behavior. If only we had admitted our stupidity we may have been forgiven. Needless to say, the cookie episode left everyone with a bitter taste not for one, five, or ten years, but for many more decades. We still aren't sorry!

We're quite certain that some readers may think to themselves, How absurd and childish can people be because of soda and cookies! However, if you honestly look at some of your own quarrels with your 20s child, you may be astonished to discover that with few exceptions your quarrels begin with trivia. The residue of bitter feelings comes not from the initial incident but from the escalating anger and the generalization to a lot of other things.

An argument may start out with sodas, move quickly onto leaving the kitchen a mess, take a giant step forward with slurs about carelessness with possessions, include further accusations about total disregard for money and failure to see that money doesn't grow on trees, and conclude with references to long-distance telephone calls.

It is imperative that a parent do whatever he or she can to short-circuit an argument that may have begun with trivia. Once the spiraling takes off, negative feelings become harder and harder to check. In some cases years can pass, wasted years because the parent and child are at swords' ends. The rifts grow wider with time and eventually become a chasm that can never be bridged.

Someone has to break the vicious circle right at the start. Someone has to initiate the cooling off and cooling down period. Only then can a rational discussion of what is troubling both parent and child be possible. And, perhaps, at that point it may not even be worth rehashing.

We're strong advocates of forgiving and forgetting. Parents instinctively do this when children are small. We're sure that if your 6-year-old son left a favorite toy in the backyard and the toy rusted, you didn't bear a grudge against him years later. Although the truck was expensive, it is doubtful that you dragged up the rusted truck as strong piece of evidence against your son every time he was less than perfect. Remember you are the parent no matter whether your kid is 6 or 60.

IT'S TOUGH FOR PARENTS TO LET THEIR KIDS GROW UP

"My daughter is 23, temporarily working in California," one mother told us. "She came home for Christmas and didn't bring one warm jacket. She grew up here in Wisconsin and knows our winters. She went out in an unlined leather jacket. I wanted her to take one of my coats. She told me she wouldn't be caught dead wearing my down jacket."

"'Stop nagging me to wear your clothes. They're not my taste.'

"'It's not a matter of taste. It's a matter of being warm.'

"I told her one of the parental rights forever was a right to nag. I really was joking. The exchange left a bitter taste for the rest of the holiday. How could I let her go out dressed like that?"

If her daughter shivered in Wisconsin freezing temperatures, that was not mom's concern. Once a parent, always a parent, but the nature of parenting must change. It's not going to be easy.

"What do I do," asked one mother, "stop mothering because there's a birthday and 19 has become 20? My feelings haven't changed just because another year was added to my son's life."

Because of their great psychological investment in their children, some parents find it very difficult to let go. One mother was bluntly told, "Mom, you've got to get a life."

Just as kids change when they turn 20, parents change. We think we're the same individuals. This is far from the case. However, recognizing signs of aging in ourselves is not all that easy. Old family patterns, ways of behaving and relating die hard. It's hard to shift gears. For example, when you have a teenage child, you're accustomed to handing out directives, giving advice, making your opinions explicit. If parents are the mainstays of financial support, their power is great. Even though parents may have the best of intentions, the kindest of motives, the most generous of spirits, when it comes to parenting teenagers and younger children, there's no question who are the commanders-in-chief.

After a child is 20 the small inquiries, the minor nudges, the subtle and not-so-subtle disapproval about things that are none of our business can only lead to discontent. It's one thing to know that you should let go and reinforce your child's independence. It's quite another thing to behave accordingly.

No longer pals and best friends

"Once a year my son and I took a camping trip together. We really were buddies. I have great memories of sitting around a fire at night talking with him. During college he didn't have time to take trips. It was a couple of years before we could make plans. He was 25. It struck me how quickly the years had passed.

"When we were packing our gear he said something about how much this trip obviously meant to me. I admitted it. What I couldn't bring myself to tell him was how hurt I felt. He never said one single word about what the experience of being together meant to him."

When our younger son was growing up, he was Joel's tennis partner. "I always wanted a built-in tennis partner," was one of Joel's standard remarks. They played tennis together throughout our son's childhood. After 20, the time between tennis dates grew longer and longer.

When our son was in his late 20s visiting us, Joel eagerly suggested a tennis afternoon. The magic was clearly gone. Our son sneaked periodic looks at his watch.

Throughout the 20s, occasionally playing games with a parent, from frisbee to tennis, from camping to mountain biking, will be tolerated. It is highly unlikely that 20s kids suggest these family outings. Parents could save themselves a lot of hurt feelings by remembering never to bring up the subject for discussion.

There is no need for despair. Raising kids involves learning how to let go. Remember when your child first entered kindergarten? Holding hands, you walked to the school entrance. The child darted inside the building. Long after, your hand still felt warm from your child's tight clasp; your stomach churned with tension until the end of that school day.

Parents knew it was time to let go just as they knew when it was time to hand over the car keys and let a child drive solo in the family car. Throughout childhood and the teens, parents continue to practice letting go. These rehearsals are important lessons, not always easy for parents to learn, much less to accept. By the time kids enter their 20s, it is important they move on both physically and psychologically. They're no longer parents' best friends or the best companions for camping adventures.

Naturally parents feel a loss. There's absolutely nothing wrong with feeling nostalgic. The danger is in overreacting. We assure you that this psychological and physical separation of the 20s is temporary. Don't forget, you've got a lot of parenting years waiting for you in the next decades.

Things are going to change. Look upon this distancing in the 20s as a little relief time. You need it to energize yourself for the years ahead. Someday you may be sitting night after night in a stuffy cabin on a cruise with your mid-30s kids. They've asked you to babysit their six-month-old while they dance away the nights. You will think back longingly to the happy free time you had when they were in their 20s.

So let the 20s run off and play volleyball games on the beach with their peers, go on fishing trips with their pals, play tennis with their boyfriends or girlfriends. We urge you to make reservations at a nice restaurant with people your own age!

PUTTING YOUR DREAMS, DESIRES, HOPES, AND WISHES FOR YOUR KIDS ON HOLD

"All my friends' daughters are planning weddings. My daughter is 28. She's starting a new career. Before she begins this job, she's off with a group to India. They're staying in a Buddhist monastery."

"I told my 27-year-old son he could start taking over the family business. I'll be there to help him. If an opportunity like this had been offered to me at his age, I would have jumped. I had to make my way from scratch. He doesn't have to start at the bottom like I did. I know a lot of kids his age would give their right arm for this kind of break. My son? He wants to be an actor. It's a crazy idea."

Everybody's child but yours grooved nicely.

Everybody's child but yours graduates from college and eagerly jumps at a chance to enter dad's or mom's business.

Every daughter but yours is married with one child, another on the way, a full-time career, a nanny, a lovely home.

Hearing these kinds of wonderful stories is particularly hurtful to a parent who may not be exactly thrilled with a son who spends hours strumming a guitar. Tales of wonderful accomplishments of other people's daughters are painful to the parent whose child is depressed because of a broken engagement and the job she very much wanted that wasn't offered to her.

How should parents handle feelings of discomfort? First, keep your counsel. Say nothing about the dreams and ambitions you had for your child. Second, do not inquire about friends' or relatives' children the same age. If people are insistent about recounting their kids' exploits, we suggest you break off the conversation by remembering a pressing dental appointment.

Think of yourself when you were in your early 20s. What were your flights of fancy? Where did you want to run? What dreams did you dare to dream? *A big dose of empathy will help you get through temporary glitches in your kids' lives.* When kids are younger, parents have no difficulty being empathic. Hurt feelings, a broken heart, an upset in school, a game lost, and parents naturally respond. Somehow after kids turn 20, we expect them to face life stoically. Grin and bear up under the unpleasant. The message parents send explicitly or implicitly is that you are not a little child anymore. Grow up. Big kids don't cry.

There's nothing inherently wrong with parents thinking their kids should grow up and not be coddled. But we also feel home should be a haven, the cave a kid can crawl back to and feel safe and secure in with supportive, reassuring parents. Moments of needing the security of family, a home base, and accepting parents will occur throughout life, not only in the 20s. *Your few well-chosen words and gestures of support at any age are going to make all the difference. Children are children forever.*

It will never hurt for a parent to say, "I know how you feel," whether the child is 20 or 50-plus. Your kids may not admit or show they care about your evaluation, but your opinion *always* counts. When kids are in their 20s, it's hard for them to imagine that their parents have concerns and worries about their welfare.

We take a little child on our lap for hugs and whispers of "I love you. Everything is going to be all right." It's not done with older kids. And yet we honestly feel that expressions of parental love, interest, concern, and respect are important for kids at any age. There is no glow that quite equals the pleasure kids feel with expressions of parental love and pride, even if they would never in a million years admit to having these kinds of feelings.

THE NEW ALLIANCE

A new epoch in parenting begins when a parent is no longer the significant other family member in a child's life. Spouses or live-in companions take over this role. Parents may not have noticed, but for some time they haven't figured much in the 20s' thoughts. Marriage or a live-in arrangement is simply a kid's public statement of "letting go" from the nuclear family.

Parents often sense a loss. They may try to console themselves by putting a positive spin on the change. They interpret a marriage, for example, as a gain of a new son or daughter. Parents seldom consider the fact that the new addition to their family might perceive them as falling far short of their expectations. Besides, they already have a perfectly good set of parents. The last thing they need or want is a second set.

"'What shall I call you?' my future daughter-in-law asked me," reported one mother. "At 26 she's already on an executive rung of the corporate ladder. She's groomed to perfection—hair always in place. Clothes straight from a fashion magazine— scarf around her neck, trouser pants with a knife crease.

"We were sitting in the yard. You have to imagine the scene. I had been gardening. I was wearing old jeans, my husband's discarded shirt, and a beat-up straw hat. 'What shall you call me?' I repeated. A mess, I thought, wisely keeping my mouth shut. I told her to make her own decision about what she felt comfortable with."

Twenties males don't think much one way or another about in-laws. Future fathers-in-law probably aren't badgering them about what they should wear at a wedding. Future fathers-in-law aren't taking them to lunch, throwing showers, having them sit down and make out guest lists and pore over the style of wedding invitations. After the marriage, it's no big sweat on occasion to sit with the father-in-law watching football on a Sunday afternoon and having a beer.

A 20s daughter-in-law is much more on guard, wary, cautious, a little on edge with a mother-in-law. She's another female in competition for her future husband's affection. She's also someone the couple had to ask, willingly or not willingly, about a guest list and choices of entrées for the wedding dinner. Common courtesy demanded this consultation.

After the wedding a wise mother-in-law will fade gracefully from the scene and stay in the background until she earns enough points of good behavior to be part of the picture. The reality is that even with the best of intentions, there's a little bit of cat-and-mouse playing. The 20s are especially cagey about their territorial rights.

If the prospective daughter-in-law or son-in law doesn't measure up to your idea of a dream spouse for your child, you can take comfort in the knowledge that out of the scores of interviews and surveys we completed, rarely did a parent of children who made independent choices of spouses say, "My daughter/son is going to marry exactly the kind of person I would have chosen for her/him."

The reason for this is that parents childishly hang on to preconceived notions of whom their kids should marry. Deep down, parents see their kids as special people, therefore, the significant other in their kids' lives has to fulfill an overwhelming list of specifications. Twenties parents have a knack for evaluating everything including: race, religion, values, education, style of dress, social class, weight, height, and even size. "My son is a beanpole. His bride is twice his size," lamented one discontented mother. "She told me she was planning on going on a diet for the wedding because she wants a beautiful wedding picture for the mantel."

Parents of 30s kids, for the most part, tend to be somewhat inattentive about the characteristics of an intended spouse; mothers and fathers of 40s and 50s kids not only inattend but will stare sternly at anyone who has the audacity to make personal inquiries. Who your son or daughter marries is far less important as long as your child is happy.

One mother commented, "I cared deeply who my daughter married the first time. She was 23. I think back and the concerns I had now seem childish. When she married for the second time, she was 45 trying to raise teenaged kids without any help. My reaction was that all of us won the lottery with the guy even though I still can't tell you the color of his eyes."

REMEMBER TO KEEP SMILING

Smile when the person your child marries falls short of your expectations. Smile at whatever wedding plans are made. Smile more broadly when your inner tensions are the highest. Unless you come from a culture where parents choose the bride or the groom, it is highly unlikely that you will be consulted about a child's choice of a spouse. Smile and get on with it.

Please don't underestimate or dismiss our admonition to smile, because if your child plans a traditional wedding with all the usual events before the wedding, you must keep that smile. Even the most benign of families somehow encounter bumps during this period. Wedding plans can get very involved.

Accept the reality that from now on you are no longer central in your son or daughter's life. The chosen spouse takes over that position. Learn to move into a back seat—take your place on the "back burner" of your child's family life. If parents of adult children were given quizzes and asked, "Now that your child has married, who should be the person central in your child's life?" we know every one of you, including ourselves, would ace this quiz. We would answer correctly, "The spouse."

However, knowing this intellectually and really feeling it emotionally may be different. Parents must recognize that it is important for a couple to establish themselves and their respective families as independent from parents. Your job as a parent is to foster this independence wherever and however you can.

While it is true in some cultures that a daughter-in-law has to pay obeisance to the mother-in-law, it is simply *not* true of the American culture. Today more than ever, women have their independence and are not going to defer to a mother-in-law, nor do we feel they should. All you can reasonably expect is politeness or courtesy. Anything more will be a bonus.

No matter how great you think you may be, the road to happiness between in-laws and daughters-in-law/sons-in-law is bound to be paved with potholes. More often than not the problem will be between the son's mother and the daughter-in-law. There are, of course, two sides to every in-law story. As one mother-in-law said about her daughter-in-law, "If I am the no good, horrible person she makes me out to be, how come she chose to marry my son? I assure you he wasn't some kind of flower who grew up in the wild. If I am this miserable creature, how could it be that I raised someone she thinks of as her dream guy?"

It might also be helpful for mothers-in-law who are less than ecstatic about their daughters-in-law to ask themselves, "What is it about this girl I am having problems with? She must have some special qualities, or my fantastic, wonderful, handsome, intelligent son would not have married her."

REASONS FOR TENSIONS BETWEEN DAUGHTER-IN-LAW AND MOTHER-IN-LAW

Dissension that inevitably occurs on some level between a mother-in-law and a daughter-in-law is a consequence of the fact that the new daughter-in-law must establish her turf or property rights. The property is the spouse. The new wife must assert herself, establish her territory.

Anything a mother-in-law does, from an innocent telephone call to an unannounced visit (the worst sin of all), can be experienced as an invasion of a daughter-in-law's territory. Thus, it is incumbent upon a mother-in-law during this period of establishing territorial possession to take a big step backward and smile. Turf wars can never be won—at least by a mother-in-law. Back off from day one.

Recognize the need for a daughter-in-law to be the *supreme commander* of her house. (If you are having trouble with this concept, think back to the early days of your own marriage.) Give that daughter-in-law choices. Give her chances to refuse to come for a holiday dinner even though you have the defrosted turkey ready to be cooked.

"Of course," you say, "I totally understand. Your parents are having the whole family over and will be heartsick if you don't show up." Smile. Hang in there. Be patient. Especially during the initial territorial struggle for dominance you will be tested time and time again.

Never say anything, do anything—give your opinion, but be the person in the wings. *Let time do its job and it will.* We promise a bright golden day in the future. "You know, dear mother of my husband (or whatever you're called), I never thought I'd like you. But I do!"

"From what you've said," one mother commented, "it looks like I am always going to be a guest in my son's house."

A guest does not presume intimacy in the private life of a host or hostess. A guest is unfailingly polite, respectful, considerate. A guest does not barge into another person's home without being invited. A guest respects privacy. And, therefore, our answer to this woman's thoughts about whether she will always be a guest in her son's home is an unequivocal, "Yes!"

WHAT ABOUT RESPECT TO PARENTS?

Young people aren't hung up or concerned about the problem of respect. *It is our contention that one has to earn respect. Nothing is really due us.* Parents are not an exception.

Respect will mean a lot less as you get older. How much respect does a person need anyhow? What really counts is the warmth of a greeting, acceptance, a cheery and honest hello, and a "happy to see you" attitude. We believe parents should keep their eye on the prize, which is the quality and strength of their relationship with their children and their families.

Don't think of a positive relationship as a battle to be won. Have a short, selective memory when less-than-pleasant incidents occur. Of course blow off steam in private, *never* to friends or other relatives. Gossip travels fast.

Never pout and have hurt feelings when a daughter-in-law tells you all about the reshaping and remolding she has had to do because of the inadequacies of your parenting job. A daughter-in-law does have to claim her rights over your son, but she also has a second job (in her opinion), which is to undo the awful wrongs you as a parent committed. In countless ways a daughter-in-law will have to modify, change, socialize, revise, transform, shape, and mold her new possession into the image she sees as the perfect spouse.

For example, we, as parents, were failures at teaching our two sons how to dress properly with style and elegance. Both daughters-in-law quite independently came to this conclusion. Defensively we say that times are different, styles are different, and perhaps Joel failed to keep up with the latest trends.

Don't be shocked as we were when your sons, whom you thought of in baggy pants and stretched-out sweatshirts, turn up at your door in classic three-button suits, starched shirts, and smashing, incredibly expensive ties. Just smile. You may even like the new product! *We did!*

THE 20S END WITH A BANG, NOT A WHIMPER

The 20s don't wind down. As the 20s approach their 30s, they seem to get a second wind. It is obvious they are far more energized at the end of the decade than they were at the beginning. This change is undoubtedly a function of their being more focused, less all over the map, with feelings of being more in control of their lives. They certainly are more conscious of their futures.

What about your parenting? You've learned a great deal. We're confident that you developed the knack of withholding your judgment and opinions about sensitive issues no matter what you privately thought. You've realized that you might not have all the answers that you once had when your kids were in their teens.

And last but not certainly least has been your increasing awareness that the social and economic world your kids live in is vastly different from the one you experienced. This last realization is perhaps the most critical lesson parents can learn. It will make a huge difference in relating to one's kids when parents face this reality. All of us who grew up in a different era have had to deal with adult children's choices in all areas of their lives that may seem foreign to us.

Coping with changing social mores and behaviors certainly hasn't been all that easy during this decade. It's been particularly difficult, we know, when your kids have challenged traditional values in everything from choice of a significant other to ways of conducting their lives. It's far from easy for parents of 20- to 29-year-olds to have everything familiar turned upside down.

By this time in your parenting career, you have gained increasing patience in the face of your adult child's trials and errors. You have acquired some healthy insensitivity to the trivial ups and downs of your 20s child's everyday life. And you have learned to focus on the loving relationship between your child and yourself, rather than on any other goal. You are now ready for parenting your 30s child.

THE SETTLING THIRTIES
Parenting the Adult Child From 30–39

ONE DECADE DRAWS TO A CLOSE. ANOTHER IS DAWNING.

Take a deep breath. You've had some experience parenting 20- to 29-year-old kids. That will certainly help as you begin parenting 30- to 39-year-olds. Although you feel you have gained some knowledge, and we agree you have acquired experience, it is important to avoid feeling smug. The temptation to assume you have all the answers is great; however, there are many things yet to learn. It will be helpful if you think of the lessons of the past decade as a good, solid, introductory course.

Remember after you finished raising a toddler, how competent, self-assured you felt about your parenting skills? Think back for a moment. Was the knowledge you gained of any real use when you began coping with teenagers? Didn't that bewildering age make you once again feel like a novice parent?

We draw this parallel simply because we want you to appreciate that the parenting skills you developed in the 20- to 29-year-old period can only do so much toward helping you manage 30- to 39-year-old kids. This period of life introduces a whole new set of problems for both you and your children. There are going to be many times you will feel like a first-time parent with a newborn.

While there's nothing intrinsically wrong in enjoying a momentary lull of calmness or a sense of security because you feel able to cope with a lot of different situations, guard against complacency. At all times be prepared for surprises, shocks, and, last but not least, a great deal of pleasure if you are willing to heed advice.

ON TOP OF THE WORLD BEFORE REALITY SHOCK!

Parents of 30- to 39-year-olds by and large feel on top of the world. They look at their children and see healthy, young, vigorous, busy, active kids, who have jobs of one sort or another. Most important of all, most kids have moved out of the house, taken the last book, field hockey stick, old pair of ice skates, basketball, or bicycle. They live in their own apartments or in a newly purchased or rented home.

Parents with children this age think to themselves, "I can unwind. I've made it through the confusion of the 20s, the agonizing self-doubts, the upsets and 'what am I going to do with my life' kinds of questions. I look at my kids now and feel they're really adults.

"In terms of problems, my parenting days are over. I'll sit back and enjoy them, relax. If they're married, I'll hope for grandchildren; with the singles, I'll scout out a few prospective candidates; if they've selected another lifestyle, I'll adapt. Perhaps it's time for me to get in a few rounds of golf, think about retiring (depending on your age), or enjoy my job (for those still actively working).

"There's so much to be thankful for. I count my blessings. The son who was going to be a standup comic is off in another direction. A daughter has a new promotion. Another son has finally found a great new job he really enjoys. A new daughter-in-law told me she was the luckiest woman alive because I was going to be her future mother-in-law. A son-in-law hung a big mirror for me. He's very handy around the house. I totally accept the radically different lifestyle of my oldest child. His (or her) significant other couldn't be nicer to me."

We hesitate in bursting these fantasy bubbles. After some of the anxieties of the previous decade, parents deserve a temporary peaceful break. However, we strongly encourage preparedness and thinking about the future.

Therefore, return to your seat on the roller coaster of parenting; buckle the seat belt; sit back. Being forewarned will make life easier, smoother, and happier for everyone. Your 30- to 39-year-olds will be especially grateful for your understanding. They won't have to contend with worried looks or furrowed brows when they tell you about what's going on in their lives.

MAJOR DEVELOPMENTAL TASKS

Having waded through their 20s, perhaps doing the singles scene, shifting jobs, snorkeling in the Caribbean, spending a summer or two as a groupie in a shared beach house, the 30s decade is one of settling down and getting into a groove. Singles start thinking more about serious dating. Some women may skim through magazines featuring weddings. Right from the start of the decade, and for the next several years, most single males judge women in terms of their potential as a spouse.

For women, the first rumblings of the biological clock begin. Many years ago we did a study of women turning 30 and had an unprecedented response to what we identified as baby hunger, every woman's longing for a baby. Our discovery was that the desire for a baby has nothing to do with an intellectual craving but rather is an emotional, biological desire. This desire prompts single women who have purposefully postponed marriage in their 20s to actively begin husband hunting starting about 30. Prospective candidates are evaluated not only for their earning potential and lovemaking skills but for qualities that might make them good fathers. Married women who have put off having children in their 20s also think babies. Statistics bear this fact out. When compared to the 20s, the boom in births is astonishing.

THE START OF THE NESTING STAGE

The major developmental tasks of the 30s involve raising a family or planning on having a family in the not-too-distant future. We shall call this the nesting stage. Those who postponed getting married in their 20s march to the altar in droves. As thoughts about starting a family sprout, couples suddenly look at what they once might have thought was a spacious apartment and decide it is much too small. No place for a baby that may not even have been conceived. Buying a house is the logical next step, and this means curtailing extras. Suddenly the splurge on vacations becomes less important than stashing money away for a down payment.

Thirty- to 39-year-olds don't cringe at the idea of settling down. In many cases they eagerly welcome the change. Running out every night, going to singles gatherings, eating at chic restaurants becomes a repetitious bore. How many new charming Bengali restaurants can you find in one week? How many cups of coffee can you drink at coffee bars while having intense discussions about something or other?

Thirties recognize they have outgrown the swinging 20s; e.g., going to bed at dawn and sleeping through Sunday. They get up early and go to aerobic classes or jog. Their newfound feelings of maturity prompt many individuals to look back at some of the funky things they did in their 20- to 29-year-old stage as "prehistoric ways to get pleasure."

Backpacking in southern France and sleeping in a haystack no longer seem deliciously charming. Certainly the last thing they want to do is repeat a summer tenting experience complete with mosquitoes and burnt backs on some island that doesn't even have a decent takeout deli.

For both men and women, careers are taking off, or show possibilities. Generally there isn't as much job searching and job shifting as there was a few years back. Current positions are given a chance. For the most part, changes are made up the ladder in the same line of work. For example, a 30- to 39-year-old woman isn't likely to leap from being a ballet dancer to becoming a high-tech computer jock.

We do not by any means suggest that 30- to 39-year-olds are dullards, settling in conventional ruts. What the age does enjoy is some sense of stability, a desire for a place in society. Generally speaking, a place in the larger society is a reward for more or less conventional behavior. Thus, 30s men and women meet their increased financial demands, fulfill their community obligations, and maintain some social life with a familiar crowd. There is a new sense of self-importance. They march for causes, participate in school activities, not in a rebellious way, but rather in a way to benefit the larger society.

Peers become important, and there is an increase in "home" entertaining, developing a social life, building a network of personal and professional friends. Parents may hear the following apology, "Mom, we know it's Dad's birthday, but can we change the date? We've been invited to the Sloans for dinner. Don has to show up. It's important for me. Sloan told Don that he's invited someone I should meet. A great opportunity for me to join a marketing team."

People in their thirties are busy, involved, on the go, running from commitment to commitment. Outsiders may look at this age as an exhausting, impossible way to live. It seems like there is too much of everything going on in their lives.

"I can't believe my daughter's schedule. A job, babysitters, a social life, a book club, and the gym. Her husband is just as busy with the kids, taking them to school and delivering the baby to a daycare center. They're looking for full-time help. I've had enough filling in one day a week."

In families where both the husband and wife are working, the demands on their time and energy are enormous. Careers are being established. Women are juggling chores with children, husbands, and jobs. Husbands are equally pressed for time. Many modern families no longer follow the old pattern of the wife shouldering the major responsibilities for the house and kids while the husband provides financial support.

After a maternity leave, over 63 percent of women return to their jobs. Thirty- to 39-year-old dads are not uncomfortable with one baby on the back, another in a stroller doing grocery shopping after a full day at an office.

The decade is highly intense and highly active. Fortunately, 30- to 39-year-olds feel and are still young enough to cope with the hectic pace of their lives. They have the required physical energy and stamina. For example, it isn't unusual for a 30- to 39-year-old man or woman to come home from a full day at a job, an hour's commute, and still muster up enough energy to put on jogging clothes and take a run, before sitting down to dinner.

"I LIKE MY PARENTS LIVING CLOSE TO ME. I CAN DROP THE KIDS OFF ON MY WAY TO WORK."

At the end of the 20s decade, parents of adult kids enjoy a little breathing space. Those tranquil moments soon will become distant memories. You may recall how your 20- to 29-year-olds pushed away from you, choosing not to live too close. They may have decided to work thousands of miles away to escape parental controls. It is not uncommon for 20- to 29-year-olds to use physical distancing as a way to help them gain psychological independence.

This attitude undergoes a remarkable change when 30s kids have children. Overworked, exhausted, they welcome the proximity of parents.

"We live five minutes from Mom and Dad. Dad retired from teaching. Mom is an artist. She works at home. Dad built her a studio. I can't tell you what it has meant for us to be able to drop the kids off three times a week and have my parents take over. My husband is starting a business. I have a terrific job. Two days a week I have a sitter. I count on my folks to help us out the other times.

"We're trying to hold down expenses. We just bought a home, and you know what that means with all the expenses of moving in. Frankly we chose this house because it was near my parents. I have tons of friends who envy me no end. One is devastated. Her parents are the same age as mine. They moved to Florida. I feel lucky, though lately I've been worried. Mom complains about arthritis, and she says she can't stand northern winters. Fortunately there is a lot of new medication coming out. I keep telling myself she'll be just fine."

There is no question that practical help like an extra pair of hands is important to 30- to 39-year-olds with young kids. Grandparents can babysit, provide a safe environment for after school if they live close enough. They are useful for running errands, picking up the cleaning, arranging for screen doors to be repaired.

The help parents provide their 30- to 39-year-old kids is often geared toward practical assistance. Kids value this a lot more than wise-sounding advice that they don't want anyway. If asked whether they would rather call mom about a child's problem with a teacher or have dad arrange to have the gutters on the roof cleaned, there is not a shred of doubt which would have priority.

If you are amenable and have the time and energy to provide this kind of help, 30- to 39-year-olds will be eternally grateful. "Is it my ideal of a relationship to pick up clothes at the cleaners? I kid you not. But doing little things like this makes me feel wanted—part of their lives," said one parent.

Not all parents feel so positive about being asked to help out with grandchildren. One woman said, "We have three children. Each of them has a couple of kids. If we babysit once a month for each kid, this means three weekends a month are taken up with sitting.

"Then they all like to go away. I appreciate they need some alone time. But this means a week here and there. We're on call, living at each of the houses. We can't even think about a vacation for ourselves. I'm getting flak from one daughter. She has a new baby and would like me to help out more. I wish you could hear the hints, some not so subtle, that I get. 'Mom, could you come over and keep me company?'

"I know what that's all about. She doesn't want my company. She wants to get out of the house and I'll stay with the baby. I didn't retire from my teaching to be nanny, chauffeur, cook. My husband backs off with excuses. Babysitting falls on my shoulders."

By and large women more than men shoulder the responsibilities of helping out with their 30s kids who have young children. Even if the adult kids have full-time help, parents, particularly if they are retired, are super backups who can be trusted.

THE HELP KIDS WANT FROM THEIR PARENTS DOES NOT COME WITHOUT RESTRICTIONS

The help parents provide for their 30s kids is not unconditional. Parents have to be prepared to walk a "balance beam." One woman called it a tightrope.

"My kids want us to help. This means we do exactly as they say. Even a babysitter would be able to speak her mind more than I can. Let's take last week. It was a gorgeous sunny afternoon. The kids were hunkered down in front of the TV screen playing Nintendo, eating every kind of junk food you can imagine. It made my husband and me upset. Beautiful new bicycles sat in the garage.

"They sit glued to the idiot box. I shipped them outside— ordered them to go. When their parents came home, the first thing our grandchildren did was complain because Grandma and Grandpa made them play outdoors. My daughter said, 'Mom, please don't tell my kids what to do. This is my home. I am the mother here.'

"'And what am I,' I wanted to ask, 'the hired babysitter working without pay?'"

Another parent noted that when her kids came home after a late night when she had babysat for six hours, no one said,

"Thank you." Her son's only comment was, "Mom, couldn't you have stacked the dishes and wiped the kitchen counter?"

The children are NOT being selfish. They are so engrossed in their own activities they may forget you're not just a hired sitter. Parenting 30- to 39-year-olds who have kids will test your diplomatic skills.

NEVER VOLUNTEER ADVICE TO A 30S KID UNLESS ASKED

The first and most important rule for parents of 30- to 39-year-olds with kids is *do not* volunteer advice unless asked. If you observe your 30- to 39-year-old letting the grandchildren stay up until midnight, devour pizzas, and drink bottle after bottle of colas, just smile.

THINK TWICE BEFORE YOU GIVE ADVICE EVEN IF YOU ARE ASKED FOR YOUR OPINION. MOST OF THE TIME IT IS BETTER TO THINK YOUR RESPONSE RATHER THAN SAY WHAT'S ON YOUR MIND.

It is important for parents of adult children who are parents themselves to go through a series of steps. The first step is to assess what the child wants to hear.

Think about your reaction. What do you really want to say? If what you want to say contradicts your child's opinion, immediately abandon your thoughts. If your opinions will create a strain, they are not worth saying. Unless you see something truly life-threatening in your child's house, do not say a word.

Your major function is to provide practical help for your 30- to 39-year-old kids with families. Consider this help as a gift. Assistance, like any gift, should come without strings attached. Give freely and willingly. It might also be useful if you keep in mind that, even with the best of intentions, you may run the risk of criticism.

A 35-year-old woman who had a cesarean needed help while she was on maternity leave. The mother-in-law, a pediatric nurse, volunteered assistance.

"I decided, what better way to use my vacation time than being with my daughter-in-law when she came home from the hospital? Whatever she asked I did. She was a very sick young lady. I do think her age was a factor because she really was knocked out. Part of the problem was her physical weakness. She had to have transfusions during delivery.

"It took her six weeks to regain her strength. I was there for the first month, and during the last two weeks I went over on weekends. Whenever I could I was there in the evening.

"In all fairness, she thanked me. She bought me a present, a gold heart with the baby's photos inside. But then the real truth came out. She confided in the daughter of a mutual friend that even though I was a big help, I was terribly old-fashioned. 'Out of touch' is how she put it. She said it was probably because I went through pediatric training so long ago. Like every first mother, she was busy thinking how unusual she was because she was a mother. Yes, you're right. I am hurt. And what do I do? Go back when she needs help, I suppose, and keep my mouth shut?"

That's exactly what she should do!

MEMORIZE AND ACCEPT THE RULES OF YOUR KIDS' HOUSEHOLDS. THEY WANT TO CALL THE SHOTS ABOUT HOW TO RAISE THEIR KIDS.

Parents want proprietary rights over their kids' lives. We certainly felt that way. Nothing is more maddening than a parent saying to their adult child, "If I were you, I wouldn't take the baby out in the carriage with a pair of mittens and two sweaters." This red flag might be met with a variety of responses. "I am the parent, not you," or the jacket is whipped off and the baby's hands are left uncovered.

"Let me get the baby a screened enclosure," said one mother-in-law worried about her daughter-in-law's two huge overweight cats with unclipped claws. "Cats love milk, and they will jump on top of babies just to lick the milk. That's why there are special enclosures for people with pets like cats."

The response of the 35-year-old new mother was quite direct. She immediately went out and got another cat from the animal shelter and told her mother-in-law that cats do not like breast milk. So much for useful parental advice.

NO PRESENTS FOR EMMA!

We live three thousand miles from one son, his wife, and a granddaughter in California. We will not forget one visit when our granddaughter was about four years old. The calls started several weeks before our departure.

"Do not come out with presents. You keep asking us what to bring Emma. Absolutely nothing. Do not come with shopping bags filled with toys. How many times do we have to tell you?"

"Is there something wrong with what we buy?"

"No, but we don't want her spoiled. She has to learn that every time someone comes to the house they are to be valued for themselves and not what they bring her."

"A little present? She's only four years old!"

"You aren't listening to us. No presents."

"How will Emma feel?"

"Just fine. We have already explained to her, and she fully understands."

"So when we come in empty-handed after not having seen her for some months, she will be very happy?"

"She will not say anything, and she will be happy."

The loud and clear message, repeated in any number of calls and e-mails, took some time for us to accept. Our son and daughter-in-law were adamant. Under no circumstances were we to violate the "no presents" rule. Reluctantly we obeyed, wondering what we would say when she asked us about presents.

Our response would be, "Grandma and Grandpa have come to see you. Our presence should bring more than enough pleasure, far more than some silly Barbie doll you love or the dollhouse we had in mind. Be thankful for our love and kisses."

And her response, if she followed the parental scenario, would be, "Oh joy. That is exactly what I, a four-year-old, adore from grandparents. I did not want a Snow White video, a Barbie car, or a princess dress. Those are only material objects and not worthy of my interest." She is an exceedingly bright child (all grandchildren by definition are), and she would respond exactly as she had been drilled.

The day of our arrival came. We rang the doorbell and, as the parents predicted, we were greeted with hugs and kisses. And then with that duty finished, Emma, grinning from ear to ear, clapped her hands and asked, "Now my presents!"

"We don't have any presents." We hadn't the heart to give the rest of our prepared speech.

"No presents." The smile faded slowly. "In your suitcase?" Her voice quivered. The lower lip trembled.

"Nothing, Emma. Nothing in our suitcase." We advisedly kept silent about love or about how our presence should be intrinsically rewarding, far more so than mounds of plastic from the Disney stores or silly items from her favorite haunt, Hello Kitty.

"Not even one little present," she whispered sadly as we tucked her in bed. She held up one finger. "Don't you have any money to get me a present?"

The rule had seemed all wrong to us; however, when we thought about it from our kids' point of view, the no present decision made sense. It was awkward if every time someone visited she expected a gift. No one enjoys visiting a home where the first words of greeting from a child are, "What did you bring me?"

However, we wondered if we couldn't be exceptions! Fortunately our kids had seen their daughter's disappointment and came up with a superb compromise solution. We could take Emma shopping at the mall.

We had a great day at the Disney and Hello Kitty stores. Two shopping bags were filled with plastic. To Emma's credit, her tastes were, for the most part, moderate.

"I like it when Grandma and Grandpa don't bring me presents when they visit," she told her parents. She wondered if we could go shopping every time we came. Actually, there was less risk. If she chose the present, we could be certain she would like it.

Parents have their reasons for rules. If you can work around them with the compromises they suggest, so much the better! If not, just obey the rules without commenting.

EVERYTHING YOUR 30- TO 39-YEAR-OLDS DO OR SAY IS 100 PERCENT RIGHT—FOR THEM

It's so very tempting for parents to hand out advice to their adult children about parenting techniques. Just remember that whatever they do is 100 percent right for them, just as you and we thought everything we did was 100 percent right for our kids when they were small. If you remember that parents have all the answers, you will never run into any problems with your adult kids, most particularly daughters-in-law. With your own children, there may be occasions when words of advice will be tolerated. Just make sure you play it safe and come forth with your pearls of wisdom only when it will really make a difference.

A RESURGENCE OF PROTECTING ONE'S TURF

The first few years of your kids' marriages is generally smooth sailing in terms of family relationships. Parents and in-laws bask in the glow that spills over from the honeymoon while the couples delight in each other's companionship. We suggest caution. In-laws run the risk of letting down their guard, relaxing a little bit, and maybe saying what's on their minds.

For the most part such slips won't matter too much except after a baby is born. Mothers who may have felt pangs of rejection suddenly find their adult daughters calling and making contact. This can be a shock to parents recalling these very same daughters who, in their early 20s, bent over backward to assert their independence.

The advice seeking of your 30s daughters will be short-lived. After the baby is about six months of age, there will be a dropping off of consultation, and when the grandchild begins nursery school, even that may vanish. Parents should enjoy the increased contact in those early months and not think about the future.

"I enjoyed calling my mom and talking to her about the baby," said one 34-year-old new mother. "It's not that I needed the advice, but I think she enjoyed having me ask questions. I could count on her being interested. That's for sure."

"MY DAUGHTER-IN-LAW THOUGHT I NEEDED MORE EXPERIENCE HANDLING HER NEWBORN SON. I ONLY HAD FIVE KIDS OF MY OWN."

The last person a daughter-in-law turns to is a mother-in-law. If anything, the chasm widens after the birth of a baby.

"I was visiting my daughter-in-law and my new grandson," one mother-in-law reported. "I've always thought of her as a lovely woman. She's 37 years of age, home on maternity leave from a very good job. Jimmy is her first child.

"The child was lying on the floor on a special baby quilt. There were at least a dozen toys, more than any three-month-old could possibly play with. I kneeled down to pick him up.

"'No,' she screamed. 'You're doing it all wrong. I would really prefer you left him there. It's his play time. There are special ways to hold his head. Cup the head here, support the neck, the spine.'

"I was given an anatomy lesson of babies. She was very definite. I was not to pick up the baby. Perhaps when he was older, and I had more experience, it would be okay. I did not pick up the baby. Perhaps I could use more experience. After all, including her husband, I only had five kids."

"Does reading to a newborn help SAT scores?"

The behavior of 30s parents is strikingly different from cavalier 20- to 29-year-olds. Younger mothers have no compunction about popping a baby into a sling, going off to the movies or Starbucks to meet friends. Babies are not fragile creatures. If mothers want to blast rock music at baby's naptime, no big deal. Babies adjust to parents, not the other way around.

Thirty- to 39-year-olds are far more tentative. They join baby classes, read, and buy a vast assortment of books on every conceivable subject of managing infants, from how to adjust voice levels to the amount of exposure to classical music six-month-old babies need. "Will reading to a baby make a difference?" asks the alert 30- to 39-year-old.

The behavior is understandable. By and large 30- to 39-year-olds, particularly those with a first child, may have married late. A first child is a carefully planned major event. The baby may not only have a special nursery but the home is outfitted with intercoms and monitors of various sorts. The slightest unexpected sound, burp, or cry spurs the 30- to 39-year-old into action. A young 20s mother will get cotton for her ears.

Recognizing the sensitivity of the 30s mother, parents must tread cautiously in handing out advice. The 20- to 29-year-old welcomes parents. It doesn't matter if the grandparent who's supposed to babysit has a red nose and sniffles; he or she will be welcome. The young 20- to 29-year-olds know a baby has a built-in immune system in the early months. Getting out of the house for the young mother is more important than a few sneezes. With the 30- to 39-year-olds, a red nose is worse than a red flag to a bull. Even after the symptoms disappear, when you visit, wear a surgical mask.

It's not that we suggest that parents of 30s kids retreat from the grandchildren, but we do strongly urge obedience to any and all directives. If the mother says stand ten feet away from the crib and says, "Don't stare right at the baby because the baby's eyes may cross," be sure to stand the ten feet away and say, "My, I have so much to learn."

We assure you that as the 30- to 39-year-old first-time mother gains confidence, she will relax. Let her learn from her peer group, the stack of books on her shelf, the baby classes she attends. Don't gasp when she tells you the baby is doing well in swimming and can now float face-down without any support. That class was expensive, and swimming, we all know, is excellent exercise.

"But it is my grandchild, my first," one mother of a 37-year-old woman told us. "I've waited so long for this child. I'm dying to hold the baby."

"Did you make sure you washed your hands with a disinfectant as your daughter-in-law told you to do?" we asked.

"Of course. She still had some excuse about the baby having trouble burping after meals and she needed to stay twenty minutes on her stomach with her head to one side. Some nonsense or other."

Avoiding all hassles will have its rewards. We promised the parent that if she hung back, followed orders, she was going to be pleasantly surprised in the next decade by a phone call.

"Is there any chance you can babysit for us this Saturday night? John and I haven't had one night out since the baby was born and it's my fortieth birthday!"

HELP YOUR KIDS LEARN HOW TO HAVE FUN WITH THEIR KIDS, NOT TO TAKE EVERYTHING SO SERIOUSLY

We were summoned to the principal's office when our second son was about three years old. We were responsible 36-year-old parents. Arriving promptly for the conference, we sat in apprehensive silence. Our son's classroom work and his teacher evaluations were spread out on her desk. She intently studied the impressive collection of charts and reports.

"It is the opinion of the staff that you are making too much of an effort to enjoy your son. Your lighthearted, carefree style is doing him a disservice, to say nothing of the effects of this kind of casual attitude when he grows older. I recall your behavior with your first child. You weren't at all the way you are now—smiling and laughing."

She was absolutely right. We could not deny her observations. Our first son was born at the start of our 30s decade. Typical of 30s, we had taken on the responsibility of being parents with deadly earnestness. Reactions of the baby were monitored. We consulted books. There were several famous studies that documented what a child should be doing at practically every month from birth on. We checked the contents regularly.

Parenting was a serious undertaking. Was the baby touching his or her toes at six months? Did the baby turn pages of a book and pretend to read? The list of observations to check was awesome. Because of our chosen profession, psychology, we got trapped into microscopic analyses of our child's behavior.

"You've changed," said the principal.

Embarrassed, we nodded in agreement.

"Just as an illustration of your less-than-serious attitude," she droned on, "let's look at your son's meteorology report for the week. Why don't you compare his work with what his classmates turned in."

Our son had brought home an assignment sheet. He was to chart sunny days, draw clouds or raindrops on the rainy days, and read the thermometer on the door. Everyone in the class had to buy a thermometer. At the end of the week he was to make weather charts. There was a model to follow. The report he handed in was pathetic, a mess of scribbles in colors with paste globs (his idea) to represent fat raindrops.

All the children in the neighborhood attended this nursery school known for its excellent preschool curriculum. It wasn't anywhere up to the standards of a good Japanese school for kids the same age. If we had been living in Tokyo, he would have not only monitored the weather but would have been able to make graphs in centigrade and Fahrenheit.

The weaknesses of his meteorology report were surpassed by those of the botany project. Even we could see that was awful. We hadn't had much time that evening and handed him scotch tape. He had taped parts of leaves over nearly half a ream of paper. Everything had been scribbled over with stripes of different colors.

"I don't want you to think I am comparing, but it will be helpful to show you what children his age are capable of doing with parental supervision. Your not having time is no excuse. All the parents in the class have demanding careers."

Not even bothering to conceal names, she displayed other youngsters' work. We studied enlarged cardboard thermometers, charts, graphs of the week's weather. There was even a printout of enlarged raindrops. However, Janie G., whose father was a professor of botany, had really outdone himself. Each leaf page included a miniaturized photo of the tree. The leaves were all labeled with both English and Latin names in stunning Gothic script.

In our effort to loosen up our child-rearing tactics, we had made the mistake of laughing our way through the assignment. First there had been a game of catching raindrops on our tongue. That was really silly. Collecting leaves had been wild. We threw the raked leaves at each other, stamped on them, and then, when we had enough, our son collected a few torn scraps and scotch taped them to paper. The best part, of course, was the scribbling of lines in every color.

In our society there is a tendency to emphasize the serious side of parenting. From the principal's perspective, we were irresponsible 30s parents. Our effort to change was not met with approval. Not one other member of our peer group had any sympathy for us when we recounted the story. Our next door neighbor, a media engineer, had just finished a recording complete with a soundtrack for his eight-year-old. The assignment for his third grader was to interview a family member.

The seriousness of the educational process makes sense to 30- to 39-year-olds. They are serious people. This is an age of doing, productivity, career building. Drainpipes in the house have to be cleaned, storm windows purchased, car repairs made, and concerns about stashing away retirement monies must be addressed. These are hardly laughing matters.

Laughter with kids? Play with the kids? These are foreign concepts. A town in New Jersey recently designated one night a week as Family Fun Night. No TV watching. Only Family Fun. The newspapers featured photos of families going to libraries, sitting around playing Scrabble. For the parents, fun night with the kids probably seemed just one more burden to be added to already hectic schedules.

HOW CAN PARENTS OF 30- TO 39-YEAR-OLDS HELP?

Parents of 30- to 39-year-olds can provide an invaluable service. They can help their kids see *there is fun in having kids*. They can help the parents loosen up, lighten up, and have fun without town ordinances directing them to do so. Family life can sometimes be far too serious for harassed 30- to 39-year-olds. Dual jobs, endless obligations, career concerns, pressures coming every which way may stop lighthearted laughter from surfacing. While there are many aspects of the lives of 30- to 39-year-olds that parents can't do much about, they can, at least, provide some healthy perspective on life.

This is where your maturity and experience will make a difference. By the time you're parents of 30- to 39-year-olds, you've probably learned not to take everything in life so seriously. You can provide some levity, a laid-back attitude, and most important of all, a sense of the fun of living with kids.

THE INEVITABLE FEELINGS OF REJECTION THAT COME WITH THE DECADE

By the time your kids enter their 30s, you've had varying experiences of feeling rejected. For the most part, those instances when you felt slighted were within acceptable limits.

Kids not calling, failing to visit, not speaking very much when they did come didn't really bother you too much. Parents of kids in their 20s tend to be quite accepting of a lack of good manners. This is because, in their opinion, 20s children are more or less overgrown teenagers, and we all know what that age is like.

Teenagers don't remember to tell their parents where they are going and what they are doing. They have to be told to thank grandparents for generous birthday checks. They don't clean up after late night snacks without reminders. Thus, the lapses in politeness and attention to parents that occur in the 20s are a familiar pattern.

Parents don't expect a 24-year-old daughter, for example, to call mom about the purchase of an incredibly expensive pair of shoes unless she wants mom to contribute to the cost. A 26-year-old young man is not likely to tell mom or dad about the smashing new woman he met at a singles bar the previous evening.

"I think they do care that I'm alive," joked one mother. For the most part, parents are most accepting that busy 20- to 29-year-olds do not have time. By and large the attitude is, "If I don't hear from them, I know everything is fine. If there were problems, my phone would ring constantly." Parents of the 20- to 29-year-olds deep down are delighted their kids have busy lives, even if it means fewer calls and visits.

"HE NEVER ASKS ABOUT US"

There is a not-so-subtle change that begins in the 30s decade. While parents are aware that their kids have tons on their minds, from careers to family concerns, they may become terribly bothered when children do not make contact with them on a regular basis.

Worse than infrequent contact is the lament of one mother about her son. "He calls. He never asks about us. Oh yes, he asks how are we feeling as if we were some medical case, but really meaningful questions go unasked. As far as he's concerned, I suppose if we're healthy and financially okay he has nothing to worry about. The conversations are so bland."

This is quite true. Chances are that by the time you are parents of kids between the ages of 30 and 39 you are anywhere from your late 50s on up. If you are in the upper ranges of age and are thinking of retiring, your kids may worry whether you have enough money. Helping you financially is an expense that is less than appealing. If you're sick, that could really pose a problem for them.

If you've already retired, the typical 30- to 39-year-old is not going to be terribly excited about who was elected or not elected to the condo board, who was present at the last bingo game, or who entered the oldsters, golf tournament. Social security, Medicare, retirement plans, or any of a dozen other age-related concerns are of no interest. And, finally for you parents who are still working, chances are that unless you're in the same occupation, your job concerns or activities aren't going to excite the interests of your 30- to 39-year-olds. The kids are right. There really isn't much to talk about.

THIRTY- TO 39-YEAR-OLDS LIKE TO KNOW YOU'RE FINANCIALLY INDEPENDENT AND HEALTHY

What 30- to 39-year-olds do care about is that their parents are independently functioning and not a financial burden. With all the expenses 30s already have, from home costs to planning ahead for college tuition to paying child support or alimony, the last thing they want is to have to worry about their parents. If everything is going well with their parents, they are grateful not to have one more concern. A little reassurance on this score will ease their minds.

We urge parents of 30- to 39-year-olds to graciously accept their decreased role in their children's lives. Don't think of the behavior as active rejection because they are paying less attention. You are probably lucky because you aren't immediately needed to help them economically or with assistance in other ways. Knowing that the reason for not being in touch is because they are busy will take the edge off those moments when you feel terribly sorry for yourself.

So what if the phone doesn't ring on a regular basis or there are far fewer visits than there were in the previous decade? We assure you, when they need you, they will call. One woman who hadn't heard from her 34-year-old son in weeks was pleasantly surprised with an unexpected stream of visits and calls.

"Mom, I need your help."

Her son had started a catering business. One Saturday afternoon Joel and I were on a busy Broadway corner near the discount theater ticket booths. Our beautifully groomed acquaintance passed, arms filled with bright yellow flyers. She marched up and down the queue. In a strong, appealing tone she told each person in the line, "I'd like to tell you about a new sandwich shop. The food is delicious. I should know. My son is the owner. He makes them."

DON'T BOMBARD YOUR CHILD WITH PHONE CALLS

In those periods of long silences, just relax. Attend to other chores while you wait to be asked to help plan a wedding, baby-sit, come up with cash during a cash-flow problem, share some of your furniture because they know you are or at least should be thinking about downsizing. Whatever you do, curb your temptation to initiate telephone calls.

In the past, when the phone rang, if people were home they answered the telephone. Caller ID, we fear, has changed the ease parents once had of guaranteeing a chat with their 30- to 39-year-old kids.

"No one ever answers," one mother told us. "It's strange. I can't imagine he's out day and night. Perhaps he's taking a shower and doesn't hear the phone."

We did not have the heart to tell this mother about Caller ID. Rather than run the risk of not having your call answered, being cut off because there's another call waiting, or hearing lame excuses such as, "We're in the middle of dinner, we'll call you later," *don't call*. Learn to wait. You'll be a lot happier. We assure you calls will start coming more frequently at the end of the decade. So somehow hobble through the 30s years knowing the future holds rewards.

BE GRATEFUL FOR THE TECHNOLOGICAL AGE

Memories of kids returning home from school, sitting around the kitchen table having a snack, teenagers getting ready for proms and soccer games, warm summer Sunday evenings hanging out in the backyard after a barbecue—these are typical sentimental parental thoughts which trigger off an urge to make contact with adult kids of any age. Many parental telephone calls are prompted by these flashbacks of memory.

After the long silences in the 20s years, desire for contact picks up when kids turn 30. Of course, if you have a good reason to call, that is a different story. The troublesome calls are those that occur impulsively as a result of nostalgia. Mothers more than fathers are more likely to make calls at that time. They really don't have any specific thing to say. "It's just hearing my daughter's voice," explained one mother, "that makes me want to call her." The content of the conversation doesn't matter in the slightest. It was the mother's way of reaching out to contact her daughter.

WHEN THE URGE TO MAKE CONTACT BECOMES ALL-POWERFUL

When parents experience these waves of feeling, we urge them to stop right in their tracks. Rush to your computer; turn on your e-mail; send a message. We guarantee you 100 percent increased contact with your kids when you begin to use e-mail. You may only get one or two lines in return. The length is of no consequence. What is important is a response and the signing off with "love" at the end of the message.

Thirty- to 39-year-old kids are accustomed to sending and receiving e-mails. They read their e-mails. They will read yours. Send them reminders. Send them suggestions telling them to make sure they put weed killer on the lawn if that's what you feel like telling them. Tell them you love them.

There are, of course, those parents who would criticize e-mails as impersonal. "I want to hear a voice," said one parent. "You lose so much when you are reduced to typing a message."

Loss of the intimacy of a voice is a reality, but everything in life is a tradeoff. Think of the absence of vocal communication as a plus. It's not so easy to put hurt feelings in a written message. In fact, none of the parental annoyances from anger to irritation will show up. What will appear and what will count for more than anything is signing off with love, "Miss you," which is what you really wanted to say anyhow.

Any downsides to an e-mail message over an actual voice are far outweighed by the advantage of being able to reach out to your kids at ridiculous times of the day or night. A phone call made at the same impossible hour would be a disaster. We've written e-mails in the middle of the night, at dawn, in the afternoon. And our reward is, at some point, they are unfailingly answered. It's the way of the twenty-first century.

"THANK GOODNESS FOR MY SON'S LONG COMMUTE!"

It is doubtful that creators of cell phones had parents in mind when they developed the technology. But parents of 30- to 39-year-olds should express their gratitude to the inventors.

"There was a time," said one parent, "when I felt sorry for my son having a long commute. In a traffic jam, he can be stuck more than an hour. I blamed his wife. She was the one who made the decision of where they were to live, never thinking about what this meant in his life.

"No more. Her idea was great. I get to talk to my son at least three times a week. We talk until the battery runs low."

Another parent reported that her 38-year-old son calls nearly every evening at around seven, something he never did.

"His wife has to drive the sitter home. My son takes a walk with the baby. I have a feeling he's bored, so he calls me on a cell phone. I hear the latest about the grandchild or whatever. I hear more from him than I have in the past ten years."

Hopefully your kids will have long commutes to and from their jobs. Traffic jams, train delays will work in your favor. There will be other times, like driving sitters home, or waiting in line at grocery stores, that you'll receive unexpected calls. That will be nice because your feelings of rejection will disappear.

We personally like to make it a point to be home between 6 and 7:30. Coincidentally, there have been major road repairs on the east and west coasts. Our kids discovered that talking to parents is a nice way to while away the time. Parents don't object to hearing gripes about road conditions as long as they can speak with their kids.

BUSY 30- TO 39-YEAR-OLDS CAN FORGET THEY HAVE PARENTS; PARENTS NEVER FORGET THEY HAVE KIDS

"I sometimes think my son has forgotten he has a mother," complained one woman. Her son hasn't forgotten. She is the one who has forgotten how busy her son is. Of course, any age is a busy one. Thirty- to 39-year-olds, though, are a little hyped up after the 20s when they were more laid back. Later, in the 40s, they will be more organized. Right now they are on the move and may respond with a private groan to parents' demands for attention.

What is dangerous and unproductive is parents misinterpreting the behavior as rejection and falling into a pattern of obsessing about being dropped from their kids' lives. Even worse is engaging in attention-getting maneuvers. "My mother's migraines and my father's arthritis, which never affect his golf game or her going out with friends, has not won them one drop of attention," commented one 39-year-old. The lesson to be learned is, whenever you find yourself being caught in the spiral of feeling sorry for yourself because no one has called or visited, remember to send an extra e-mail!

THE LOSS OF EVERY HOLIDAY EXCEPT YOUR OWN BIRTHDAY

"Thanksgiving was always our holiday—a family holiday. When my kids got married a few years ago, everyone came to our house." This mother reminisced about cooking turkeys, fresh cranberry sauce, and home-baked pies. "I may not be a great cook, but I outdid myself for Thanksgiving. Everybody enjoyed the day at our house."

Of course they did. The children were in their 20s. One of the sons was newly married. The new bride even rolled out the dough for the apple pies. It was great fun. They admired the photos recording these memorable days. Now the kids are in their 30s and the phone calls began.

"My son's wife's parents insist they come to their house for Thanksgiving this year. The mother-in-law hasn't been feeling well. We weren't officially invited, but my son said we should join them. It's only a five-hour trip. We never did receive an invitation."

The loss of holidays usually begins slowly, perhaps with Thanksgiving. Mother's Day can easily be dropped from your schedule. And Father's Day—well that is only an add-on. The 30s decade may mean one holiday after another tossed by the wayside. Easter, Thanksgiving, Christmas, Fourth of July. You may even end up losing them all.

How should you cope? Do you dig in your heels, create a scene, and insist—no, *demand*—that everyone show up at your house? Just remember, you might win back Thanksgiving one year, but you stand a good chance of losing it the next. Are you willing to fight the in-law parents if you are outnumbered or they are just plain stronger?

Are you prepared for endless discourse, telephone calls, arguments, hurt feelings, or worse yet, hints that you are being childish? After all, you could join "the other side" for the occasions. There are always good excuses. "There are more of

them. We see you on a regular basis. We do not see them."
There is no point trying to balance out the visitation demands
each side puts forward.

Learn to lose gracefully. Above all, lose with dignity. Ask
yourself, is it worth family dissension and bitter feelings that
Christmas be at your house? Remember there are plenty of days
after Christmas. And then reconsider. Why not accept the
invitations even if they are relayed through a daughter-in-law or
a son-in-law? Don't play hard to get. Accept the secondhand
invitation that you are welcome to join "the other side" of the
family for the celebration. It's worth a try.

By and large we have lost them all! At least we can console
ourselves that we have our birthdays. They can't be given away.
The important thing is not to get hurt. We promise you, as time
goes by, you may regain a holiday or two. If worst comes to
worst, and you don't, try to appreciate that there may be a very
good reason why the other side has won.

Accept your losses like a sport. You may try and be creative
and come up with your own celebrations. Some cultures have
what is called Name Days. And, if you can't be original,
remember there is Labor Day, Save the Environment Day, and
surely someone will sponsor a day celebrating Conservation of
Dinosaur Bones. Now that would be a holiday our grandsons
would enjoy.

ALPHA AND BETA FAMILIES

Parents are justifiably confused when their married kids
seem to gravitate to the spouse's family. During the 20s period,
attention to each family is pretty much evenly divided. In the
30s period, however, a noticeable increase of contact between
one or the other side may develop. This flow we have identified
and termed "Alpha in-law dominance."

The concept of alpha dominance is well documented in the
animal kingdom. For example, in wolf packs there are males
known as alpha males. They control the pack. A beta wolf bows
his head in submission to the alpha male. He knows better than

to challenge an alpha male. Rather than go into an attack mode, he slinks away and finds comfort elsewhere. In every nature film there seem to be some shots of disconsolate betas and strutting alphas. There just doesn't seem to be room for two alphas in a group.

When kids get married, more often than not, one family becomes the alpha family. They're the ones who get *all* the holidays. The betas just don't seem to be the center of the "family pack."

Rather than fret or pout, understanding the basis for alphas will go a long way toward improving your situation. For those readers who are alpha families, we encourage you *not* to skip over this section. Don't say to yourself, "Oh, this doesn't apply to me. All my kids, their spouses, and the grandkids come to our house for all the holidays." It's not that we are going to suggest you relinquish your alpha rights. An alpha wolf would hardly bow his head and give up his status to a beta member of the pack. We merely want to sensitize you to beta feelings. Perhaps you will be encouraged to include them in the next family celebration or invite them up for a weekend to the summer house.

But let's focus on why the alpha families move into that position. There are a number of reasonable explanations. First and foremost may simply be proximity. While living near adult kids does not guarantee that you will be the alpha family, it will help. You're close and available to babysit, lend a helping hand. Realistically, if you're off in a retirement community or live three thousand miles away, it's unlikely you can offer the same kind of services an alpha family living nearby can render.

Alpha families, we discovered in our survey, more than likely are larger. Let's say you have two children, one married, the other unmarried. The married couple has one little child born when the father was 34 and the mother 32. Your house isn't going to be as much fun around holidays if the alpha family, the in-laws of your son or daughter, has six siblings, each with several kids. Numbers can make a huge difference. We are going to assume that by the time you have kids in their

30s it is too late for you to have more, so we encourage you to just give up the holiday without regrets. Hopefully, the alpha family will invite you next year!

Alpha families slip into that position quite easily if they are the ones with more money. Wolves spray scents. Alphas distribute money. One mother reported in detail how her daughter was bought by what she called the "Other Side."

"Martha Stewart furnishings, designer clothing, a house in Vermont, a down payment on a house. My daughter was bought. My husband and I can't possibly match those kinds of gifts."

Money is a powerful force encouraging loyalty, attention, and fidelity at any age. This is quite understandable. A young couple buying their first home who gets a down payment from one family does feel a certain sense of obligation. This sense of obligation may evidence itself in more frequent visits. The loyalty increases as the same parents or parent gives additional gifts of patios, landscaping, furniture. It doesn't take any stretch of the imagination to see how quickly these generous parents move into an alpha position.

We are not suggesting that the alpha families knowingly mark their territories with money. They simply have spare money and are using it as they choose. They didn't go out and acquire more children just so they could have big family celebrations to make you feel sad. By the same token they didn't work harder to become richer just to make you feel less affluent. Money, kids, lots of them, perhaps a summer vacation house have all maneuvered them quite unconsciously into the alpha position. Ascendancy of the alpha family evolves slowly and naturally because of numbers and resources. They aren't necessarily intrinsically more fun. We're sure you are fun people too, but you have a few shortcomings you have no choice but to accept.

We do hope that alpha parents reading this section take their obligations and a responsibility to be empathic and sensitive to the beta group to heart. Extend an invitation when you can. Don't relay that invitation through your son or daughter.

When you have a barbecue and invite all your children, spouses, and their kids, get on the phone and invite the betas. Even if the beta says "No" at first, keep trying. Betas, like yourselves, are growing older. Initially they may act coy because they're so preoccupied being hurt and rejected that they flirt with the risk of losing perspective.

Invite the betas to the Vermont weekend house you bought for *your* children and *their* spouses so you would have a family compound like the Kennedys or the Bushes, albeit on a much less grand scale. Don't find the excuse that there aren't enough bedrooms. The weekend they come, why not go to a motel and let the beta parents have the bedroom.

Don't ever forget your alpha position is at risk. Life can take unexpected twists. You could lose your alpha position overnight. Those betas might win the lottery and the kids will follow the money trail. Thus, while relishing your role, never lose sight of the future.

For example, one of your kids might still be single. What if that dearly beloved child marries into an alpha family? You may be in for some hard times when you are unwillingly forced into a beta role. Given a possibility such as this, it is incumbent upon alphas to behave with the noblest of motives toward betas.

Beta families are definitely in more of an anomalous position. If you are a beta, keep in mind you feel vulnerable, sometimes a bit on edge, and unfortunately competitive. You sometimes stoop to such petty things as counting how many times your kids saw the alphas the previous year. However, if you stubbornly insist on such data gathering, please make very sure you do not share your findings with anyone.

You should never make any version of the following comments to your children: "Do you know how many days last year we saw you? Do you know how many days last year you spent with your in-laws? The ratio was 20 to 1, obviously not in our favor."

The presentation of such facts will not endear you. All it will do is induce guilt in your child, and, as a result, you run a risk of even greater rejection. Visitations and telephone calls may become even more infrequent. Being circumspect in what you say isn't always easy for parents accustomed to giving their opinions and reflecting their feelings. We assure you that by hanging in there, being welcoming to the kids, over time your sincerity will be recognized. "We're going to visit the alphas, Mom and Dad, but we have assigned a few days that will be completely devoted to seeing you people."

Accept every invitation from the alpha clan, even if that invitation is extended secondhand. Arrive with flowers or candy. It won't hurt if you accept the reality of a little competition. If you can't offer your adult kids and their families a Florida vacation at a fancy condo, perhaps there can be something else you can provide that won't strain your budget.

One couple whose son had aligned himself with the alpha group are artists. They couldn't match the summer retreat to a shore villa, a ski weekend in the winter condo, but they could make a number of paintings for their son's new house. They "won" nearly a whole week at Christmas. We urge betas to make the time they are allotted "quality time." If you wait long enough, your patience will be rewarded. At some point in the future you may win a whole week at Disneyland. Better yet, your photo may be posted under a brightly colored magnet on the refrigerator door.

LITTLE COMMENTS THAT CAN DRIVE CHILDREN UP A WALL

One daughter-in-law who had made a sincere effort to spend more time with her in-laws reported, "My mother-in-law drives me up a wall. I realized we hadn't been seeing my husband's parents enough. So we started to make an effort to visit them more. But when we go, the first thing she says is, 'I never see you people anymore. I guess the next time will be when the grandkids graduate high school.' Our kids are three and five. I know she's trying to be funny, but to be honest, hearing that same tired joke every time we come makes me cringe."

Avoid all the little comments and asides that may seem clever but simply serve to irritate the children.

COMMUNICATION

Do you remember when your six-year-old came home from a birthday party and you asked, "What did you do at the party? How many jellybeans did you eat?"

Six-year-olds, unlike 30- to 39-year-olds, love to give details.

"I ate ten jellybeans." Ten fingers are held up.

"I pinned the tail on the donkey." And the story goes on and on until even the most loving parent finally has had more than enough.

A few stages later, parents confront the silence of the teens.

"What did you do at the party last Saturday night?"

"Are you giving me the third degree?"

"I was just asking."

There was, if you recall, a slight resurgence of communication in the 20s decade. That was a nice surprise. You felt good hearing details about some event in your kid's life. Those feelings vanished when it dawned on you that you were only being softened for requests for help with down payments on a car or a security deposit for a perfect apartment to be shared with six college buddies. Despite your not-so-subtle hints, you did not find out what happened at a Saturday night all-night party.

In a way, communication patterns of 20s are quite similar to teen-parent communication. There's just enough information to satisfy parents' curiosity and to keep them from feeling rejected. From the parents' perspective, the limited information, though somewhat wanting, is satisfying. Parents would always like more, but little tidbits here and there are enough to assure you all is well with the kids.

Beginning with the teenage period on through 29, there is a gradual tapering off of communication. Even though you've been conditioned to expecting less, the significant drop that comes in the years from 30 to 39 is a jolt. We've cautioned you about not impulsively picking up the phone to call, to let kids take the lead in conversations, talking when they feel like it, and remaining silent at other times.

Just keep in mind there will be communication swings back and forth. What will bother you more than the amount of communication will be the quality. "It's all so different," noted one parent. "Conversations seem like shorthand to me." That is true. Thirty- to 39-year-olds do not sit down for long heart-to-heart talks with parents. For that matter, they probably don't speak that way with each other.

Several factors account for this difference. Time may not be available. With busy, active lives, 30- to 39-year-olds don't have the leisure to sit down with anyone for a nice soul-bearing session. Twenty- to 29-year-olds do this. Teenagers can spend hours grunting and sighing to each other over the phone. Thirty- to 39-year-olds are on the run.

A second factor accounting for the difference in style is the technological age. Everything is reduced to a minimum of sound bites. E-mail messages are filled with sentence fragments. Thirty- to 39-year-olds in their professional lives are used to bullets—a few condensed sentences.

"If anything is over a paragraph," one 38-year-old professional told us, "I don't bother reading the message." Speech is like a rapid-fire television commercial. A message rarely exceeds a couple of sentences. Parents who are looking for that long discursive chat, not unlike a leisurely Victorian novel, had best not chat with their 30s kids. With this group, conversations are generally information sharing—the speedier the better.

"I GET THE FEELING THE ONLY REASON MY DAUGHTER TALKS TO ME IS TO DUMP PROBLEMS ON MY SHOULDERS"

Sounds a like a pretty disgruntled mom, doesn't it? You're right. What this mother must understand is that 30s conversations are understandably egocentric.

"My daughter never asks how we're doing. As far as she's concerned, as long as her parents are alive, that's enough. She has no difficulty telling me about the baby, her job, and her tough life. She'll tell me if the hot-water heater burst and flooded the basement. I get the feeling our conversations are a way of dumping problems on me."

We're sure she is doing exactly that! Who is she going to dump her problems on? Best friends? Her 30s friends are quite capable of coming up with their own stories, perhaps not a hot-water heater, but how about an air-conditioning system breaking down on the hottest day of the year?

We're sure you remember the old game of hot potato. You passed some object around and around a circle. Someone finally ended up with the object symbolically called the "hot potato." What a sense of relief when the hot potato left your hands. That's just how kids feel after unloading their problems onto parents' shoulders. Let mom or dad sit and obsess about the hot-water heater, air conditioner, and flooded basement.

By the time parents have kids between 30 and 39 years of age, more than likely they are expert worriers. A few more things won't make their lives any worse. Kids surely feel relieved. They've dumped their problems on parents and can now have a cocktail and go out for dinner.

Do you really feel your relationships with 30- to 39-year-olds would be better if you could tell them about problems you're having, such as getting social security payments straightened out, the lawn mowed, thinking about whether or not a neighbor had a heart attack or another had new heart valves put in and he was only 63? Nonsense, you wouldn't feel any better.

IMPROVING THE COMMUNICATION BETWEEN PARENTS AND THEIR 30- TO 39-YEAR-OLDS

Despite what parents may think, they have considerable potential skills and power to improve fading communication between themselves and their 30- to 39-year-olds. The first step is to remind yourself they are busy and have a ton of things on their minds. Thus, when you do get called or have an unexpected visit, show pleasure, but don't lose control.

For example, don't fling the door open and smother them with kisses and hugs. Thirties are somewhat sensitive about excessive physical contact with parents. There are others in their lives who are on the receiving end. In this sense there is a throwback to the teen years. You will recall how teens couldn't take parents "crawling all over them." Twenty- to 29-year-olds are less concerned. They hug and kiss practically everyone. However, 30- to 39-year-olds may visibly react negatively to outrageous displays of hugs and kisses. Be patient. We assure you there is a revival of kissing and bear hugs when kids move into their 40 to 50-plus stages of life.

Our second suggestion has to do with questioning. From the day a child learns to talk, parents become expert interrogators. By and large they adhere closely to the "5 W" format, indispensable to journalists.

What did you do?
Where did you go?
When did you go?
Who did you go with?
Why did you go?

The vast majority of 30- to 39-year-olds on the receiving end of this kind of verbal onslaught invariably recoil.

For example, let us take a 34-year-old single daughter who makes the mistake of casually mentioning to her mother that she had a date the previous Saturday night. Immediately the mother's antennae go up. She takes a deep breath and begins innocently enough, "I don't for a moment want to ask you any questions, *but* who did you go out with? Where did you go? What did you do? Why did you go out with this person? When will you go out again?" This barrage of questioning is unlikely to elicit any information. The inviolate rule is, no matter what is said to you, no matter your profound interest, avoid questions.

It's not only mothers who are the interrogators of their children. One 38-year-old man said his dad was a past master at questioning.

"I showed him a new convertible I bought. He was very admiring. Like always when he wants to probe for more information, he goes about it in a roundabout way. With the car he started, 'When I was your age, I never could have afforded anything like this car.' He went on about the cheap little cars he could afford.

"Then he moved on to what he really wanted to know. 'Why did you by it? How could you handle the loan? What did you pay? Where did you get the money? Who else in the family is going to drive the car? When did you decide to buy it?' And then trying to soften my reaction to his inquisition he finished it off with, 'I think it's pretty nice a son of mine can have this kind of luxury.'"

No small wonder 30- to 39-year-olds approach communicating with parents tentatively. They appropriately fear being judged. They know your tastes, likes and dislikes. For example, you may be conservative and disapprove of living with a partner before marriage. Why risk your displeasure and tell parents details about your living arrangements that will make them miserable?

We've had parents contradict us, insisting that nothing in today's world could possibly surprise them. They would accept anything their kids told them. Their only resentment is not hearing any confidences.

"I never tell my kids what they should or should not do," said one woman. "They could tell me anything and I would be fine."

In speaking with her children, however, we heard a slightly different story. "It's true, Mom never says anything judgmental. She doesn't have to. If there's something she doesn't like, watch her face. The mouth gets set. Her eyes narrow, her lips purse, and she stands ramrod straight. She starts this awful throat clearing, and then she storms out of the room, slams the kitchen door."

Conversations between kids and parents, and this includes in-laws, can also grind to a halt with effective conversation stoppers even when the intent might be positive.

"My mother-in-law complains because I tighten up and never say anything to her. She's right on. She knows I like being thin. She also knows I was once ten pounds heavier. The first thing out of her mouth when I come into the house is, 'Annie dear, you've lost weight!' She beams."

In a tactful moment we were able to speak with the mother-in-law. From her perspective, she was being complimentary. She knew her daughter-in-law liked being thin. It was hard for her to understand that the daughter-in-law went ballistic being constantly reminded of a past she wanted to forget.

THE IMPORTANCE OF NONVERBAL COMMUNICATION

Parents can't assume the only form of reacting is verbal. You may be preventing your kids from telling you anything because of a whole range of nonverbal cues. For years we studied nonverbal communication. Our research demonstrated that emotions could be accurately communicated by the nonverbal aspects of language.

The simple sentence, "I am going out this evening, I'll be back and will call you later," could be said in a way that could communicate happiness, hate, fear, anger, despondency, sadness, and so on. It was often said that the famous actress Sarah Bernhardt could recite the alphabet and reduce an audience to tears. Thus, what you say may have far less impact than the manner in which you say it.

It is a tightrope, isn't it, having to be on guard with the content of your speech as well as your style of speaking? You're probably thinking to yourself, "All this advice is going to make me tongue-tied." After years of studying parent-child interactions, we've concluded this might not be such a bad idea.

Caution on your part will make you a better parent of 30s kids. This age group is sensitive about their independence, standing on their own two feet. Putting a hold on some of your thoughts, particularly when they touch sensitive areas, and not letting your true feelings come through nonverbally will be most important in surviving this decade.

There are specific techniques that will help in your communication. The first is borrowed from a nondirective therapy technique. With a minimum of practice you can acquire enough skill to serve your needs.

Your 33-year-old son comes to visit. He slouches in a chair, picks up a magazine, scans a few pages, and tosses it aside. Leaning back, eyes closed, he mumbles, "Life sucks."

A concerned parent might leap into action with a barrage of questions: "What happened? What's wrong? What can I do? What do you need?"

Most likely this approach will elicit comments such as: "You can't stay out of my life, can you? You want to know every detail." The magazine will be slammed down, and the child will leave the room in a blaze of anger.

Now let's look at the same situation using a nondirective approach.

Remember the comment, "Life sucks"?

In a quiet tone, you say something like, "Sometimes life can really be tough."

"Yeah," the 33-year-old replies.

"You're feeling miserable."

"Yeah, I sure am."

Little by little, adding just a shade or two of comments, always in a nonjudgmental tone, you reflect the feeling your child expressed. Within a short time, your child will begin to open up.

"You have no idea why my life sucks," says the child.

"No idea, not one idea," you reply.

"Well, I'll tell you—" and the whole story pours out.

Be careful not to make invasive or judgmental comments. Stick to reflecting as best you can the feelings expressed. In other words, focus on what is important, the way your child feels rather than how you feel, what you're curious about, or your idea for a rapid solution to the problem. Guard against a tendency to overtalk, adding bits and pieces of advice or sneaking in a few questions. You can be most helpful to your adult child by showing that you are primarily concerned with how he or she feels, without being in the least judgmental or controlling. You will be amazed how this kind of reflective, empathic listening will do wonders for communication between you and your 30- to 39-year-old.

COMMUNICATION QUIZ

We'd like to end this communication section with a quiz. You are free to take the test as often as you like. This is not a timed test. Take as much time as you need to think about the correct answer. Do *not* proceed to the next sections until you obtain a 100 percent score.

1. You walk into a daughter-in-law's house on a Sunday morning. A four-year-old is seated at the kitchen table having a bowl of chocolate ice cream with sprinkles and gummy drops. A two-year-old is on the floor with a big stalk of green broccoli in one hand gnawing a Snickers bar.

You say (choose only one answer):

A. "Chocolate ice cream in the morning! That's awful! And the baby with that Snickers bar! Do you have any idea what your kids' teeth will be like if you give them that kind of diet? I never, never allowed my son to eat junk food!"

B. "That broccoli has a beautiful green color. How clever of you. Did you buy it at an organic food store? Gummy drops! Lucky, lucky you. Can Grandma have a gummy drop?"

2. Your 35-year-old son arranges to bring his latest serious love over to meet you. The couple walks into the house. She has **TWO** heads!

You say:

A. "How could you do this to your parents? Where did you find her? You can't possibly be seriously thinking you'll marry this woman!"

B. "How lovely to meet you." And to your son, "One brunette and one blonde. How ingenious you are!"

3. Your 37-year-old son and his wife have decided to buy a summer house. They take you to see it hoping you will help with the sizeable down payment. The house is a fixer-upper without a furnace, windows, or working plumbing. Floors in each room are cracked flowered linoleum. The couple is clearly enchanted.

You say:

A. "What kind of a damn fool idea is this? You can't be serious. This place is a wreck. So the yard has a couple of trees. They look dead to me. What is in you people's minds? Give you money for this? You must think I'm insane."

B. (You go up a rickety flight of stairs to the second floor. Looking out of a windowless opening, you close your eyes so you won't see the gas station across the road and say,) "The view must be lovely in the spring when the trees that are living have leaves."

4. Your 39-year-old daughter is entering a second marriage. She has asked you to help plan the wedding. It will be on a beach with everyone getting a chance to windsurf, and there will be a sandcastle contest for the guests.

You say:

A. "Windsurf at my age! Are you mad? What do I wear—a flowered bikini with a skinny spaghetti halter-top? Does your father wear a skintight pair of briefs? I can see myself with rubber gloves trying to protect a manicure while digging holes in the sand with a shovel. I can't wait."

B. "How original a wedding plan, darling. This is the first time I will have gone to a wedding and dug a sandcastle! Everything's a first in life, I always say. Windsurfing—what a marvelous treat at my age!"

The correct answers are all Bs. Check your score sheet. If you have 100 percent, you have mastered basic communication skills for talking to 30s children. We must warn you, however, there will be modifications you'll have to make in the next decade. Nevertheless, we encourage you to relax, knowing you've made one giant step in the right direction.

HANDLING DIVORCE

The rate of divorce escalates in the 30s decade. Of course, divorces occur in every age group. However, for parents of adult kids, divorces of their 30s kids may impose greater stress on parents than kids divorcing at other ages.

Why might this be so? With the 20- to 29-year-old age group, recovery from a divorce is often fast. After a brief mourning period, they're back in the social swim again, particularly if they are childless. Early short-lived marriages, generally under five years, have recently been portrayed as "starter marriages." Kids get a chance to practice marriage before really settling down with a lifelong partner.

Everything changes in the 30s decade. First of all, the individuals are more serious about everything in life. Splitting up with a partner, whether the marriage has lasted one year or ten, can be traumatic. If there are children in the marriage, the pain, hurt, and psychological damage can be overwhelming even if the marriage was dissolved without apparent rancor.

"My daughter is 36. She moved back home with a 2- and a 4-year-old. I keep asking myself, 'Why did it happen?' I can't get her to talk about the problem. I had no idea the marriage was headed in that direction. If only I had seen signs, I would have done anything to stop their breaking up."

Really? Done anything? That is unrealistic wish fulfillment. Parents cannot blame themselves. Unfortunately, there is usually very little parents can do to stop a child's marriage from going downhill. Watching kids go through the pain of separation and divorce takes its toll on parents who may have come from generations where divorce was not viewed as a solution to marriage incompatibility.

One father told his son, "You don't back out when the going gets tough. Everyone has problems. Don't for a moment think your mother and I weren't ready to throw in the towel with our marriage. We didn't split."

The son's answer, the father reported, was blunt. "I'm not you. Maybe you and Mom made a mistake, the way you people sometimes fought."

Parents will discover that kids who divorce are not very interested in parental commentary about their decision. It is wise to hold one's counsel.

The pain of divorce is equally hard on parents who themselves are divorced. "I can't understand my daughter. She knew what it was like watching me go through a divorce. Now she's repeating history. Like mother, like daughter, I suppose."

Parents should not assume that kids who opt for divorce have made a cavalier decision. Divorce today is viewed as a natural way out of problems. Statistics note that one out of two marriages ends in divorce court. The hard part is for parents empathizing with their kids' unhappiness and, in a number of instances, being put in the position of having to offer financial assistance and psychological support.

One mother reported, "My son was crushed. His wife walked out on their marriage. It wasn't that they had rushed into getting married. They were both 34 at the time. He's now 36. Two years later she leaves. He insists there wasn't one word of warning.

"She told him she found someone else. I asked him, 'How could that be? You were newlyweds. You just furnished the apartment.'

"First he told me, 'None of your damn business.' Then he said it was someone she had gone with when she was in college. They met by chance after the guy got his divorce.

"He's moved back home with us. First, he said, 'No.' I left the offer open, and he came back home. Not to stay but to recover. You know my husband and I stay home at nights. I just feel he needs someone in the house. We don't always socialize, but when we have late snacks he comes out to join us. We're there for him. He knows this."

While there isn't much this parent can do to help her divorced kid over this rough period, there are a number of things parents should avoid doing like the plague. The first is checking up on the divorced child's social life. One mother of a divorced woman who walked out on a marriage regularly calls her daughter to see if she's met anyone.

"I make all sorts of suggestions. She won't listen. She tells me she's miserable. Why won't she join a singles group? I find myself looking at strange men to see if they might be eligible. I'm going crazy because of her. I know she's lonely. Every suggestion I make is like waving a red flag in her face."

No matter the age of the kids, parents have no choice but to keep mum about the marriage. One mother has deeply regretted what she said. "I blamed my daughter. I really think it was her fault. I never saw her act decently toward her husband. She treated him like he was a doormat. I understand where she's coming from—a liberated woman. But the poor guy, and he was a sweetheart, never had a chance.

"My grandchildren even said to her, 'Mom, Dad's new girlfriend never talks to him the way you did.' My daughter was married at 25 and divorced at 39. There are two beautiful children. They're not happy. Their dad's new girlfriend is the age my daughter was when they first married—25. She's seven months pregnant, and the wedding is next month. It breaks my heart. My daughter is alone. What man is going to look at a 39-year-old woman with two kids?"

All the conventional stereotypes of a woman's role and a man's role seem to emerge in the wake of a divorce. There is blame all around. And for parents with divorced kids, the temptation to take sides is very compelling. No side taking, no comments, and you'll do your kids a big favor. Just help out how and when you can.

One woman was caught in a real bind. "My son left a beautiful woman for a bitch. I'm sorry I have to speak that way. The first wife was an angel. She couldn't have been nicer to me, to everyone. That was her way. I could go on singing her praises. I worry sick that my son will find out that I am still in contact with her. I've bought presents. I would do anything for that woman."

We certainly would not for a moment suggest hostility or any sort of unpleasantness toward a first wife; however, we wonder about the reaction of this woman's son if he discovers his mother's relationship with his first wife. Don't lose sight of the fact that your first allegiance is toward your own child, no matter what.

TERRIBLE TWOS REVISITED

In many ways the 30s is a comfortable age for parents simply because, by the time your kids are somewhere in this decade, you're a little older. Chances are you're less frivolous than you were a few years or so ago. The serious tone of your kids sits well with you.

However, we just don't want anyone to settle back assuming all will be serene in the relationship. The Terrible Twos Revisited can pop up at any time. This is true, of course, for kids of all ages, 20 to 50-plus. However, with the 30s, Terrible Twos can be a bit stronger.

Remember the Twos with foot stamping, blaming mom and dad, rebelling at restraints? Heads shook in little tantrums and not-so-little tantrums. The worst people were mommy and daddy imposing restraints, directing their behavior, not giving them what they wanted.

Well, be grateful for this early experience. When the Terrible Twos Revisited pops up at any age, you won't be shocked. You will understand. Mom, dad, or both can be blamed for everything. The blame can be about anything, whether you suggested the family come for dinner, made a comment about the way the patio was built, or told them their vacation plans sounded a little extreme or that letting their kids have six Cokes before dinner was not a good idea.

You may be blamed for things you did in the long ago past. Of course, dredging up the past is a popular sport for any age kid, but it is particularly popular for the 30- to 39-year-olds who may be feeling some discontent in their own lives or who may be getting flak from their own children. This is especially true if their kids are teenagers, less so if the children are younger.

One mother was blamed because she had wide hips, a broad bone structure. "My daughter told me she has my figure, my metabolism. If she doesn't watch it, run to a gym a couple of nights a week, she's afraid she'll spread like me—her mother."

One mother described how her son felt she was an embarrassment to him. "He lives in a beautiful loft in Manhattan. I am divorced, have to support myself. I've never gotten a cent from my son's father. It's true, I don't have beautiful clothes. I live in a studio apartment. It hurts very much to hear the way he makes fun of my lifestyle."

In some instances Terrible Two behavior can erupt with an innocent comment on your part. Kids don't realize that parents sometimes prattle on just to have some "noise in the channel." They want some kind of interaction. For parents, interaction generally means verbal exchanges. Thus, walking into a 39-year-old's house and getting a grunt acknowledging your presence might prompt you to say, "What's the matter, don't I get a kiss?"

If the day hasn't been perfect or there are lots of important things on the kid's mind, the Terrible Two behavior might just erupt. "Can't you ever just come into my house without a comment?"

It was hard for one father to believe that his son, 37 years of age, blamed him for not having taught him about the business world. "I grew up in the depression," said the father. "We were damn lucky, when I was a kid, to have food on the table. My kid grows up in luxury I never knew, and he tells me he remembers when all the kids in his high school had cars except him."

Surviving the Terrible Twos Revisited is not going to be difficult if you keep in mind a few guidelines. First of all, never forget to keep your head when your kids are losing theirs and blaming it on you. Don't stoop to blaming in return. Don't defend or apologize because you did not give them a convertible when they were in high school or you have a lousy metabolism and a weight problem yourself. That's life. They'll have to tough it out.

Your role when the going gets a little rough is to maintain your cool at all times. Continue to be pleasant, praising, and nonjudgmental even when you have judgments. On occasion play a little hard to get. Let your kids and yourself off the hook once in a while. Every holiday, every birthday, Sunday afternoon picnics, including the Fourth of July, shouldn't be a must. You don't have to retreat to an extreme; just take a little pressure off their coming to dinner, responding to your beck and call.

Kids in this decade need a breather. Just accept that the Terrible Two period is regression. Kids, of course, always go through cycles of regression with their parents. We observed a 39-year-old man losing his temper because he couldn't find his keys. He blamed his parents for misplacing them. The tantrum was relatively short-lived. The parents couldn't do anything but sit there, hands folded, staring at the table. The 39-year-old couldn't be banished from the room for a "time out" period. There was no alternative but to "sit it out." But, that's what parents are for—to blame, and a chance for kids to once again be kids.

CHANGING FAMILY PATTERNS

"I didn't lose a daughter; I gained a son." The wedding had just taken place the previous week. The young couple was still on their extended honeymoon. The mother-in-law beamed as she extravagantly praised the groom.

Very similar words were echoed by another proud mother. "I could not be happier. I'm a very fortunate woman with my new, loving daughter-in-law. She's as close to me in my heart as my own daughter. We're one happy family."

The couple had recently returned from their honeymoon, and the in-laws had been invited for a Sunday dinner. No takeout food! The new daughter-in-law who had never prepared a meal in her life had decided to cook everything from scratch. She was a busy 33-year-old executive.

We're quite sure everyone remembers Eliza Doolittle's famous words in *My Fair Lady*, "Just you wait Henry Higgins, just you wait. . . ." We definitely encourage parents to bask in the post-honeymoon glow. Why not take each pleasure in life at face value? Is it necessary to always be future oriented? Isn't it better to have blinders on than to face reality?

We wholeheartedly agree with these kinds of attitudes; however, we suggest that somewhere in the back of your mind you remember to prepare yourself for the inevitable reality shock. The myths that you are gaining new sons or daughters when your kids marry must be dispelled, or you will never be able to enter a productive relationship with the new spouse of your child.

When your kid marries, the configuration of your family dramatically changes. First of all, your child's allegiance, as it should, begins to shift steadily and surely toward the spouse. Don't delude yourself into thinking you can move in on that dyad, nor should you. The best that you can hope for in the beginning is cordiality and peace. The next step in the relationship can be anything from an armed truce to downright hostility. And last and most important, warmth and real friendship may develop if you follow our suggestions. This is particularly important for parents of kids from 30 to 39, much more so than from 20 to 29.

Twenty- to 29-year-olds dance to their own tunes. If they don't see eye-to-eye with their in-laws, they say to themselves, "Tough luck for them," and go off in their own direction. If they don't want to sit through a boring Sunday dinner listening to pop-in-law go on and on about his last fishing trip, they walk out without a look backward.

On the positive side, 20- to 29-year-olds have short memories. This is a blessing. Because they quickly forget their rudeness, they are more than willing to have pop- and mom-in-law show up the following week with wicker baskets filled with goodies. In this respect, 20- to 29-year-olds share teenager sensibilities. They can be sullen and obstinate one minute and delicious smiles and hugs the next.

Although the issues and problems of in-laws are the same with the 30- to 39-year-olds, there is a tremendous difference. Thirty- to 39-year-olds, by virtue of their age, are less willing to compromise. They can be quite unforgiving. They're more than ready to distance themselves from the in-laws for any reason whatsoever.

Perhaps they've heard stories from friends or read books about meddlesome in-laws. Many have a stereotyped picture in their mind. Mothers-in-law by definition are troublesome. Jokes in our culture about mothers-in-law are endemic. Fathers-in-law are not immune from barbs but receive them to a vastly lesser degree. Minor stylistic differences on the part of the kids or the in-laws, once thought of as tolerable and even interesting, run the risk of becoming irritants.

GUIDELINES FOR IN-LAW BEHAVIORS WITH TOUCHY 30- TO 39-YEAR-OLDS

First and foremost, lower your expectations. Do not start off all enthusiastic, embracing this new woman or man into your family with extravagant hugs, praises about this person being the light of your life. That's totally unrealistic. You know it; the other person knows it. And soon your real self will emerge and everyone will be unhappy.

One father-in-law was ecstatic with his daughter-in-law. His son married a Japanese woman. In his eyes she was delightfully quaint, interesting, prepared marvelous food, and treated him like a king. So what if he had to take his shoes off and pad around in his socks because shoes were not allowed in the house? He just remembered to check that his socks didn't have holes in the toes; otherwise the rule was no big deal except that the two-sizes-too-small slippers she gave him to wear made him trip. However, one freezing winter day he had enough. "I will not walk on those damn cold ceramic tiles in my socks." He refused to take his shoes off. The wife pouted silently, of course. The mother-in-law remained; the father-in-law went to McDonald's.

A small incident caused a rift. But isn't that always the way? Minor things of life are the real troublemakers.

One mother noted she found it uncomfortable to have

dinner at her son-in-law's house. "He won't sit down. He brings in takeout Chinese food. The cartons are put on the kitchen counter. Everyone helps themselves. He likes a special dish, and he walks around eating directly out of the carton of stuff he bought for himself.

"That's not how my daughter was raised. The table was always set. We said grace before meals. The family sat down together. They didn't eat out of cartons and forage in the freezer for dessert before everyone else was finished eating."

In no way do we suggest that you play Mr. or Mrs. Cool. However, rather than start off with all shades of enthusiasm, try a little healthy neutrality. Show interest but not too much. If you show too much interest as a way of compensating for your lack of interest, you run the risk of being considered nosy and intrusive.

The new spouse introduced into your family may not necessarily be the gift you've been waiting for heaven to bestow. You feel happy, but frankly the person is not your ideal. Don't cover up by smiling too much. The smiles might appear as controlled grimaces. Remember, as in-laws you are always sending out messages whether they are verbal or nonverbal. The nonverbal ones, as we indicated a short while ago, can be far more potent than the verbal ones. This is why we are encouraging cautionary behavior. Think of a film going in slow motion.

Do not let yourself be troubled about the things your kid has to do to please the spouse's family. If you can't control yourself, obsess in private, never to your child. One mother was upset that her son had to make an appearance at his wife's parents' every Sunday. In this traditional Italian family, the father expected all the children and their respective families to join him for dinner. The children and grandchildren arrived early in the afternoon and remained until early evening. No excuses were permitted. After dinner the men sat in front of the TV watching sports; the women cleaned up.

The mother said, "This was unbelievable to me. My son could never make plans to visit us on Sundays. He admitted that his wife had told him about the custom before they were married. At the time it didn't seem like a big deal. I finally said to him that he was foolish for going every week. Just tell them, 'No.'

"His answer was that it was none of my business. 'This is my wife—her family.' They've never had one Sunday dinner at our house since they were married."

If you remember to move slowly, cautiously, honestly letting the relationship develop in its own way, you'll end up on sure footing. Families need different amounts of time to develop relationships. The cliché that Rome wasn't built in a day is more than apt. Decades may have to pass before you achieve a really warm healthy glow of acceptance on your part and on the part of the son-in-law or daughter-in-law. It will be worth waiting for this reward.

A LITTLE INSENSITIVITY ON YOUR PART WILL GO A LONG WAY TOWARD KEEPING PEACE

In the 20s period you began to develop the art of being insensitive to slights. In the 30s stage you will have plenty of opportunities to further hone your skills. This age can be sensitive to extreme by virtue of their being older and having had more life experiences than 20- to 29-year-olds.

Daughters-in-law are strengthening their positions. If there are children, your kids and their spouses have to learn how to be parents themselves. The roles may be very new to them.

Little by little you may find yourself pushed away from your kids' lives. You don't vacation with them. You hear about the vacations the family takes. When they start redecorating or buying new furniture, you may not even hear about the purchases. "My daughter never even told me she was getting a new roof for her house," complained one mother. Parents like to be in the know, and ignorance of the new roof made her all too aware that life was moving on with her kids without her knowledge. Of course, it's not the new roof *per se*, but it's the "not sharing" that bothered the parent.

The spouse is feeling more secure and a mother-in-law may hear more about the deficiencies of the child she raised and the need for more reshaping. Listen without comment. Daughters-in-law in the 30s are solidifying their positions. In order to take complete possession of a spouse, they have to depose the last remnants of parental influence. This process of shedding started in the previous decade. It just escalates in this stage. "It's taken me awhile," said one late 30s woman, "to get your son to wear clothes that weren't two sizes too big for him."

Do not send photos of yourself on your last vacation to be posted on the bulletin board for the grandchildren. Do not get upset if your daughter-in-law gives a barbecue for her siblings, invites her parents and your son's siblings, and leaves you out. The mother who reported this story said, "At the last minute my son called me and said we should show up. Absolutely not. I wasn't invited. I would not go."

We think the decision not to go out of pride is this mother's to make. However, we suggest that she not harbor a grudge, although well deserved, and never bring up the subject to her son. Whatever the motivation, take slights in your stride and move on.

IF YOU WANT TO BE A MARTYR, KEEP YOUR FEELINGS TO YOURSELF

The way we're presenting this advice sounds as if we're suggesting a kind of martyr-like attitude. There's nothing wrong with being a martyr if peace reigns in the family and your relationship with your child remains solid. If you don't sulk and pout, the significant other in your child's life will come around and eventually accept you.

In the meantime, boundaries are just being worked out between their house and your house. Try to think of this staking out of territory as all to the "good." One implication of this behavior is that it is indicative the marriage is on a solid footing. The spouses really care, as they rightfully should, about creating their own strong family unit. Retreat with dignity and honor while you wait out this period of distancing.

Don't call up your best friend to report the slights and barbs you may have suffered or imagined you suffered. Gossip has a way of backfiring. I vividly recall meeting my mother-in-law's best friend for the first time. After chatting with me, she turned to my mother-in-law and blurted out, "She's not the monster you told me she was."

PARENTS HAVE TO EARN A POSITIVE RELATIONSHIP WITH THEIR KIDS' SPOUSES

In some cultures the relationship between parents and their daughters-in-law or sons-in-law is clearly defined. It's not that everyone is happy, but there are unwritten rules which are closely followed.

For example, in Japan, daughters-in-law traditionally moved into their spouse's parents' homes. They were expected to be dutiful, obedient, and submissive. One Japanese woman noted she couldn't even make miso soup (a classic dish) without consulting her mother-in-law about the ingredients. Women subjected to rule by autocratic mothers-in-law had to wait their turn for revenge when they became mothers-in-law.

In some African societies, the son-in-law becomes a member of the wife's family, even going so far as to take the wife's family name as his own. Husbands obey or follow the rules of the wife's family. This is exactly what Prince Philip did when he married Queen Elizabeth II, obeying the rules of her family as to what he could or could not do. In our culture, we go to great lengths to make sure that the generations are independent. There are no established rules about how to relate to in-laws.

A solid relationship with the spouses of your adult kids is not a given. Positive relationships are earned rewards for behavior. This means going a little out of your way to be helpful and considerate, positively praising when appropriate, and above all, never taking sides no matter what.

CAN 30- TO 39-YEAR-OLD KIDS COME HOME AGAIN?

In our culture, kids have a long adolescence, nurtured until they are sent from the nest when they leave for college or enter the work world. Kids are supposed to grow up and establish their own families to be independent. Of course, we send out double messages: Be independent. Stay in close contact with your family.

What about kids who leave home and then for one reason or another return to the family nest? For that matter, do kids ever have to leave? Why leave home if home is comfortable, warm, supportive, and secure? In Italy there are laws to protect adult children from parents who try to drive their kids away from the family nest when the kids do not choose to leave.

When Italian couples marry, parents pledge to support the kids until they have fulfilled their aspirations. The constitution does not set a time limit on parental obligation. Italian courts recently supported a 30-year-old qualified lawyer's demands that his father continue giving him an allowance of $675 a month. The young man, who lived with his mother, maintained that he had been unable to find a satisfying position.

There are good reasons for adult children living with their parents. Living at home is comfortable and certainly easier financially. Japanese parents would never dream of having their adult kids contribute to household expenses. "I have my whole salary to spend on myself," commented one 34-year-old Japanese woman who was not terribly interested in getting married.

All her friends felt the same way. No one raises an eyebrow in Japan when young adults in their 30s live at home and mother makes them bento boxes for lunch. In America we push our kids toward independence. The separation process typically starts when kids leave home for college. Parents rarely expect their kids to return home after graduation.

American kids 20 to 29 years of age have no trouble with the parting of the ways. In fact, the majority feel anything is better, even a cramped apartment with too many roommates, than returning to their old bedroom. They go to great lengths to avoid going home to live.

Thirty-five-year-olds who go back home after a messy divorce with two kids or return home because of an economic downturn are sometimes met with a double message: "Glad to see you. How upsetting this had to happen."

One woman discussed her situation. "I have a 33-year-old unmarried daughter with a two-year-old. She refused to marry the father. Her excuse was she couldn't see herself spending the rest of her life with him. She told me, 'It would only end in divorce, so what's the point of getting married?' He gives her some money. She has a job, but she can't manage on her salary. It's expensive to support an apartment, nursery school, and babysitters after school.

"I retired from teaching last year. She saw me as having time on my hands and a house large enough to accommodate the two of them. And so it begins all over again. My husband thinks the two-year-old adorable. He doesn't mind in the least playing with her. The burdens fall on me. Cleaning, shopping, not feeling free. I'm back to square one where I was forty years ago when I had my first child.

"What can I do? I can't give her money to set herself up in her own home. My husband is supportive. He's still working. He can't understand what I am complaining about. I'm complaining because I'm back on duty. We were going to travel. There are a lot of things I want to do. All these plans have vanished."

How to Handle
The 30- to 39-Year-Old Child Who Returns Home

Our personal experience with a child coming home for a period of time taught us some invaluable lessons. One son returned home in his early 30s. He had made the decision to finish his doctorate degree. Financially the move home was the only way this goal could be accomplished. After not having anyone other than the two of us in the house, the shock of an adult plunged into our midst was unnerving.

Stereo sounds, dishes in the sink, a car returning home late at night, clutter—initially everything seemed like an assault on our sanity. The popular advice for people who find themselves with returning adult children rambles on about guidelines. There are suggestions for spelling out limits, rights, obligations, duties, and house rules of one sort or another. On paper all this makes sense. Adults have established routines, and when they try to live together in relatively close quarters problems are inevitable.

One advice book talked about families using a business model. Let things go slipshod and the corporation fails. Everyone will be happier with order. Magazines belong in a magazine rack. Newspapers should be left folded for the next person. Privacy is paramount. A laissez-faire household spells disaster.

We had trouble with all this advice. First of all, the idea of sitting down with our adult son and drawing up a list of rules was embarrassing. We decided to just let life take its natural course. In retrospect, we are absolutely delighted, thrilled is a better word, to say that we made this decision. What was important was our son needed the security and stability of a home at this point in his life. We were his parents. And that's what parents do—serve as a backup when needed.

The experience gave us a chance to rediscover the son who had been out of our immediate lives since he left for college at 18. He was the same son and yet so different. I learned a few new skills. A number of times he insisted I serve as sous chef. In his life away from us, sometimes in communal groups, he had learned to cook all sorts of interesting dishes we had never heard of. There were long hours we had "bull" sessions, sat around the living room, son sprawled on the floor, talking as we had talked in his teen years.

Modifications in our living? We put up a door on the laundry room—a heavy door so we couldn't hear the rumblings of the washing machine. He liked to do his laundry at unreasonable hours. It was easier to do this than to sit down and work out a laundry schedule.

I rediscovered the value of bicycle riding when my car disappeared at precisely the time I wanted to use it. Joel got up earlier and cleared the sink of dishes, a seemingly petty issue that, in fact, drove me wild. Why couldn't our son put his dirty coffee cup in the dishwasher? Did he think dishes had wings?

All the machinery of life, and it is the machinery of living, the chores that have an insidious way of coming to the foreground were ignored as best we could. What really counted was our relationship with each other. When we threw all the tacky details of living by the wayside—the petty detritus of life—we bonded more strongly than ever.

Two years later when our grown-up son left the house, and we watched the bags being stacked in the car, there was a terrible emptiness and sadness. The house seemed miserably quiet in the evening. We longed for the stereo to blast at dinner hour. What had we given up having him back with us? The list was short and kind of petty. A bathroom, the study (we moved a desk to the dining room), a Sunday morning folded newspaper. Not very meaningful when compared to what he had had to sacrifice as an adult in terms of his independence and privacy.

What had we gained by the experience? First was the recognition that adult children can come home again if they have to and need you. When they're ready to fly again, they will. And you will have the satisfaction that you rose to the occasion, found resources in yourselves you may never have known existed. Years later we asked this son about his reaction to that period in his life. Was it okay? His immediate response, "It was great." He thought it odd we should even ask about something that was so obvious to him then and now.

GETTING ANGRY AT ADULT KIDS

One memory of that period in our lives was the anger we sometimes felt. Obviously this wasn't the first time we were angry with him or with our other son. However, living together did bring about situations that were irritating to us and to him as well.

Parental anger is part of being parents. Actually, being angry at kids begins in early childhood. Every parent has experienced anger. In childhood, since parents are bigger and stronger, they are in command. Kids quake under parental displays of temper. They rarely talk back. There isn't an adult who can't recall some outburst on the part of a parent and how they suffered in silence.

The fact that kids get bigger and stronger and will talk back doesn't deter parents. They usually can shout louder than the kids. Parents fail to realize that kids get angry at them and oftentimes justifiably so. This fact rarely crosses parents' minds because parents tend to be self-righteous. They feel that when they get angry there is a good cause. If kids get angry they are being childish and obstinate.

We strongly support parental rights to lose their tempers, get angry, and verbalize the fury. It is an inalienable right of parents to feel annoyance, rage, and irritation, particularly if they feel they are 100 percent right and the kids are 100 percent wrong. There is absolutely nothing wrong with expressions of anger. It doesn't matter whether your adult son or daughter is 20 or 50-plus—if they have irritated you to the point where you are losing your sanity, by all means express the anger.

However, there is one inviolate rule we urge every parent to follow. Make sure the child or anyone else in the family is nowhere within hearing distance. Don't displace your fury onto your spouse. Find some quiet, secluded place to be *alone*. Storm, rant, shake your fist, and express anything you wish with unprintable words.

After you have vented your displeasure, treat yourself to a favorite beverage, whether it is a nice cup of tea or something a *lot* stronger. Then and only then are you ready to reenter the relationship. You will be astonished to find how relaxed you feel having let off steam. And when your kid looks at your scarlet face, a leftover from your tantrum, and inquires, "Are you okay?" you will be able to respond in a puzzled voice, "Why do you ask?"

THE END OF A REMARKABLE DECADE OF GROWTH ON YOUR PART

The 30s period draws to a close. The fortieth birthday is not unlike a graduation ceremony marking the end of an era. If a spouse has planned a party to celebrate the occasion, rejoice if you've been invited. You may be pleasantly surprised to get a call asking you to help in the planning. Perhaps you will be asked for a contribution. Why not buy the flowers, cake, main dishes, hors d'oeuvres, and the wine? Don't stint on the latter. Forty-year-olds have become wine connoisseurs. A fortieth birthday is a milestone. Whatever you can do to contribute to the event will just be another plus to your store of good parenting credits.

What's really important is you've survived. And just think of the remarkable range of lessons you've mastered. You've learned to shut up if the kids are arguing with their spouses, recognizing that whatever you said or did wouldn't have made much of a difference anyhow. If there was a divorce, you shared the sadness, loss, and bitterness such events are bound to leave in their wake.

If a new wife or husband came on the scene, you pinched yourself so you said the right name, and hopefully you've acquired enough maturity to embrace the new arrival. After all, the kids are older, but time hasn't stopped for you. With a kid turning 40 chances are you've moved into the 60s and are facing a slowing down of your golf or tennis game, if that's what you've done for recreation. You're reminding yourself to take those senior citizen vitamins in silver containers.

Everything hasn't been super about the relationship. There's been sibling rivalry rearing its head. One of your kids has accused you of paying more attention to the grandchildren of a sib more than to his or hers, but you've soothed the ruffled feelings because you've learned to be diplomatic. You would never, never say, as you may have at the beginning of your kids' 20s decade, "Damn it, I treat you kids equally. Don't ever accuse me of playing favorites."

Daughters-in-law are sweeter because you've tried a little more. By trying, we don't mean active involvement. For example, you've made an effort to call from your cell phone if you're due to arrive at 5 p.m. for dinner and it's 4:48. In fact, you probably won't even call. Instead you'll sit in the car and try to make a lame excuse when a grandchild rides by on a bicycle and asks, "Grandma, why are you and Grandpa sitting around the corner from our house? Have you forgotten where we live?"

If your kids have new girlfriends or boyfriends and have come to dinner bearing flowers, you have babbled about the stunning beauty of whatever is in the bouquet, even if its ragweed drooping over the tissue. You've learned, and we're proud of you, as we are of ourselves, for having grown wiser with age.

Don't worry about occasional lapses or regression. After all, you are human. You can't be perfect. You should not have opened up your mouth when your son told you he was taking his in-laws on a cruise because it was their forty-fifth anniversary or whatever, so he wouldn't show up at your house on Mother's Day. No way. You're an experienced parent now. You ask for the name of the cruise ship and you remember to send a box of candy for the sailing.

The 30s period is ending. You've survived beautifully and have a right to be proud. You may be disappointed because more appreciation hasn't been shown for all your generosity and kindnesses. Don't, for heaven's sake, obsess about this. It's very tempting at the end of this decade to feel sorry for yourself. You want attention. That's a human enough trait. Plan a party, but first make sure to check that everyone has a free date. Give the kids plenty of notice, and don't complain because a couple of the grandchildren don't show up.

Time to settle back. Is that what you are thinking? We certainly hope not. Just because you have survived two decades of adult kids doesn't mean you can be smug. Learning is something that goes on through life. One is never too old to acquire wisdom. Therefore, if you're due to collect social security, collect it. Take your pensions. Sit in front of the computer screen and watch your accounts, if that's what you enjoy doing. Just remember, a parent is a parent forever, and you're really ready for a whole new adventure in parenting now that the kids are 40. The next years will be a real challenge. We're confident you will sail through the storms with a smile. You will always do your best to keep your life and your relationship with your 40s and 50-plus kids on a firm and even course.

THE QUESTIONING FORTIES
Parenting the Adult Child From 40–49

Look into the mirror. Don't put on your glasses so you won't notice the worry lines. As you study your reflection in the mirror, you are probably thinking to yourself how astonishing it is that you are a parent of a 40s child. You feel like a kid yourself, and you are certain that you don't appear to have aged in years.

It's quite remarkable, isn't it, that you've survived the past several decades? Of course there were moments of great highs that you thoroughly relished. And the low periods, though disconcerting and unnerving, somehow were managed because you were circumspect and listened to good, sound advice. We appreciate that you might think to yourself, Doesn't there come a point when I've mastered all the skills I need to successfully parent?

We must disappoint you. Our reply is, not really. Life is a learning process, and this continues as you and your kids move on in years. There is a great deal more to learn. But there is a plus side. You surely are familiar with the saying that kids are great and grandchildren even greater because they keep you young! This is certainly very applicable to the 40s stage.

As you look at your 40- to 49-year-old kids, you realize how much they've changed. However, so have you. Chances are you've become a tad more egocentric, rather like the 20- to 29-year-olds. This happens with age. You're a little more considerate about yourself. You feel you are owed vacations. You are owed breaks from kids' problems, concerns. You may even say to yourself, The kids really don't need me. I've had it. I've been parenting far too long. Doesn't there ever come a time when I can say *"finis"* to the task? We're a little reluctant to dampen your spirits with some cautionary words. The parenting chores go on. Just accept the inevitable.

You're ready to discover that the challenges you faced in previous years pale in comparison to some of the issues you're going to encounter as a parent of 40- to 49-year-old kids. The kids are older. You think about words of appreciation. Kids should know enough to say, "Thank you, you're great, Mom. You're great, Dad."

We urge you not to get hung up on this need for verbal rewards or presents. If you start feeling sorry for yourself, think of your own behavior at the same age. One man bitterly complained to us that his 45-year-old kid has never said, "Thank you."

"Whatever I do for him seems to be expected. He would never pick up the check when we go out to dinner together." We hesitated to remind this gentleman that he had told us he stopped talking to his parents when he was his son's age, completely shut them out of his life.

Therefore, as you stand staring at your face in the mirror, come up with that smile that has been your lifeline in the past. Say in a strong assured voice, "How fortunate I am to be the parent of a 40- to 49-year-old child. That's a remarkable achievement. I am ready for this decade with the unbounded energy of my youth, the humor of my childhood, and the strength that comes naturally because I have a vast store of life experiences backing me up."

CHARACTERISTICS OF THE ADULT CHILD FROM 40–49

The early to middle 40s is often a time of unrest caused by a reexamination of earlier decisions and choices in establishing adult identity, particularly regarding work and choice of spouse. You recall that in the 30s your kids' noses were pointed toward the grindstone of everyday life. They were beginning careers or working devilishly hard to further their careers. Marriages were getting off to a start, or if they married in the 20s, there were kids who needed care, perhaps ready for school. With all the daily demands, there was little or no time or energy left for introspection and psychological distress.

To be self-centered and concerned about ones' neuroses, one needs the luxury of time. If you're chasing kids, going off to work, managing a house, repairing screen doors, mowing lawns, getting the backyard sprayed so you won't be eaten up alive at summer barbecues, it's unlikely that the 30- to 39-year-old has time to worry about whether his or her your psyche is intact.

The fortieth birthday celebration a spouse insists on giving may be viewed with mixed feelings. However, 40s are no different from kids at any age. There is nothing more fun than being the center of attention. For the sixth birthday party, kids wear hats. For the sixteenth, either a grunge party or tuxes and long dresses mark the celebration. For the fortieth, anything can be the theme. No presents, but still and all a vintage bottle of wine was kind of nice to receive.

Why the big deal about the fortieth birthday? Nothing was done when I turned 30, your kid thinks. Forty is a milestone of sorts, the halfway mark in life, friends quip. Forty in our culture marks the entrance into middle age. The 20- to 39-year-olds have only been practicing. Now one is really grown up and the songs go on—for you're a jolly good fellow or dame—and the 40s smiles wistfully because now society has placed an official stamp on his or her brow that the person is no longer young. No wonder there are mixed feelings—a bit of sadness at the end of that party. There's a little Peter Pan feeling in everyone.

The birthday marks a significant increase of self-awareness. The first sign is physical: minor aches and pains, a slower recovery from colds that used to be shaken off in a day, and a visit to the eye doctor. Forty-year-olds who haven't worn glasses hesitate to have that prescription filled, particularly if it's bifocals.

Getting back in shape becomes high on the list of priorities. An extra mile is added to the run for joggers, and stationary bicycles begin appearing in basements. Treadmills are added, and then a weight system. "I like to watch the cooking programs when I'm on the treadmill," said one 42-year-old woman. Aerobic classes fill up more quickly.

The second aspect of self-awareness is psychological. "If I'm ever going to make a change in my life, I better make it soon." The 40s decade begins with the first real sense of life being finite. The concept of mortality surfaces in 40s minds. "Life is all too short. I better make sure I have some fun. I don't want to stay in the same rut. Is this all there is to life? There has to be more."

These are just a few of the questions which surface in the 40s. Cosmetic companies count on a remarkable upsurge of sales with the 40-plus women. "We'd go bankrupt," said one executive off the record, "if we had to depend on the 20- and 30-year-old women to purchase our products." Forty-year-old skin needs a little prepping, smoothing, and surfacing, a little more help here and there that clear-skinned 20- and 30-year-olds don't require.

At the beginning of the decade, women may even think about menopause, even though that issue is still down the road. Career women who have postponed having children may be particularly concerned about aging eggs and the difficulties of becoming pregnant. "I waited too long," may be an unspoken regret.

The questioning of life in general spills over into the marriage, and the choice of the first spouse is questioned. Unchecked, the next step is divorce, and throughout the decade the marked upsurge in divorce rates is astonishing. The new wife, often chosen within the five years of getting out of the first marriage, may be much younger. The older 40s men find the younger 30s women irresistible. "My dad's second wife is only five years older than I am. How dare he? How can he possibly expect me to accept her?" one 20-year-old woman told us.

"I know better than to bring my date to meet my dad," joked another 20s-something man. "He left Mom. My new girlfriend is just the kind of woman he dates."

Of course there are all sorts of patterns that emerge, but the general point is that the 40s decade can be one of unrest and fantasy which sometimes turns into reality. Unrest marks this decade. Different behaviors are tried out with varying degrees. There's a lot of trial and error, and plenty of fantasy.

For any number of men and women, after a time of troubles, the psyche exploding in all directions turns toward a reaffirmation of old identity resolutions with an expansion of interests.

A restless dentist who had been in practice for about twenty years was deterred by financial considerations from giving up his flourishing practice and moving to the South Seas, as the artist Gauguin did a century ago. Instead he took up underwater photography and bought a fortune of equipment.

Divorced women feel the burst of rejection from married friends who fear their husbands will be "taken over." They begin trying to rebuild their social lives and find satisfaction in work and growing kids.

Our family had its first and only two-seated Datsun convertible in the middle of the decade. We just barely squashed ourselves into the red leather bucket seats. There was not one inch of room left over for a box of potato chips. Our teenage sons thought the purchase really cool, and if we mistakenly left the keys around, the car disappeared for the afternoon.

The decade rolls along with unexpected ups and downs, kind of like driving on a roadway with speed bumps. Just when you think you're home free and life is smooth and the car is rolling along, you're jolted back to reality.

Financial demands of the decade still remain a worry because the kids have entered high school and college expenses are not far off. However, 40- to 49-year-olds are resilient and shoulder the task of saving as just one more thing to do. "I have a double whammy," said one parent nearing the end of this decade. "I have one child in college, another starting nursery school. My daughter lives a totally unconventional life as a marine biologist diving off Chile.

"She announced she is getting married. The guy is like herself. He mostly wears flippers and rubber skin-diving suits while he watches seals. I can't believe she is insisting on a big church wedding with 200 guests, bridesmaids, and a champagne dinner dance. Her dress alone will set me back a fortune."

Parents mistakenly assumed their role as parents was drawing to a close when kids moved into the 40s decade. "When I was nearly fifty," said one man, "it never would have occurred to me to go to my folks for help. My parents would have thought something seriously wrong, would have committed me," he added, amused at the idea that at that age mom and dad played an important role in his life.

We hesitated to remind him of the past when he was proclaiming his great independence. After a bitterly contested divorce, he started stopping in to have dinner with his parents. During the early adjustment months, he spent Saturday evenings watching television with them.

A 48-year-old woman aghast that she would turn to mom and dad for advice at her age started calling home once a day, ostensibly to check on her mother's health. The woman had coincidentally just been through a painful and messy divorce. Her husband walked out of the house and married his secretary.

Parents continue to be parents in this decade, not just in the recovery period after a divorce, but for a whole host of values, from a sense of continuity, an affirmation of family, and just for helping these adult kids find out who they are and where they are coming from. No matter how old the kids, parents serve multifaceted functions.

HELPING THE KIDS GAIN SOME INSIGHT INTO THEIR UNREST

Shocked that your son is giving up his business and trying out a new career or at least talking about doing just that? We're all for parents not living in their pasts, but perhaps there are times when past memories can serve a good purpose. It's the time to search out your memory bank of yourself at the same age. Were you also planning to flee what you thought of as a humdrum existence? Did the South Seas beckon? Did you long for a different community and a chance to start over? Did you look at your wife and wonder how you married her in the first place? Did you look at your husband and recall that other guy of your youth whose name you don't even remember but who was equally attractive and perhaps had more money?

It could be any number of memories that pop up in your mind reminding you of your own desires to turn over your life and embark on something far more stimulating and exciting. Recalling your own past will go a long way toward helping you follow that golden rule of silence we once mentioned. It is important just to empathize and never to judge or nag your 40- to 49-year-old kids.

What can be useful are some helpful comments about reality. They may ease the discomfort your 40s child is feeling and help him or her get back on track. It's not that the kids necessarily really want to throw their lives over. The thought of doing so is probably just a symptom of unrest. A vacation is needed. Life's stresses are a bit too much to handle. There may be a temporary cash flow situation, problems at work. Almost anything can set a person off dreaming of escapes.

Far more important than any practical parental advice you might offer your 40s child is serving as a nonjudgmental sounding board. Here is an opportunity to practice those nondirective, reflective skills discussed earlier. You don't tell your 40s child what to do. You don't judge his or her actions. Instead, if your child does share feelings of unrest and dissatisfaction and perhaps fantasies of change, you focus on the feelings expressed and in the best way you can, show that you understand, appreciate, and respect these feelings.

If your kid does make a change and hits a brick wall, life may be tough. Don't forget that. It's not the time or the place to say, "I told you so." Those are words to be avoided at any age. The role of parents is to prop their kids up when the kids are down. What kids do not want from parents is a guilt trip, a lecture about the error of their ways. The parental function is to provide warmth, confidence, and faith.

HELPING WITH YOUR KIDS' TEENAGERS

There are endless ways you can be a rock of support. For example, your kids may have teenagers. Grandparents can be very useful in mediation between parents and teenagers. The most important benefit of age is experience, and experience gives one the levity to be rational when everyone around is losing their cool.

We are proud of blunting the edge of discord one evening in our son's house. Our grandson and his parents were having a tiff. The parents were being rather self-righteous about their behavior at the same age, a fact about which our grandson had some serious doubts. Because we follow our own advice, or try to, we sat quietly during the tirades. Our grandson at one tense moment turned to us and asked, "Was my dad all that perfect when he was a kid? Didn't he ever get into trouble? Didn't you ever explode?"

We sat composed. How should we respond?

"Our son was perfect. He never did anything wrong. He was an obedient, wonderful son from day one. We never had a cross word in our family. It was always serene. We would say to ourselves how lucky we were for such perfection."

The absurdity of our speech, delivered in stentorian tones, was enough to change our grandson's mood.

Turning to his father, he commented, "So you gave them a lot of hell, didn't you?" We quietly nodded our heads in agreement.

Short-circuiting family fights with humor can stop arguments from escalating. No family needs hurt feelings that often erode the quality of relationships. The same kind of mediation can be helpful when your kids get into family battles. A little bit of levity can help make things less monumental. Trivia can remain trivia instead of escalating into heartbreaking family ruptures.

The reward for your diplomacy and help when it comes at the right time will be the feeling of still being needed. Being needed is something that always concerns parents of any age. Discovering that 40- to 49-year-old kids still need you is a nice feeling.

This doesn't mean more frequent visits. It can mean a word here and there letting kids know they count with you and you're always there for them. You're there with psychological support when they feel out of sorts with the world, and you're there if you can be of financial help.

SHALL THE MONEY BE A LOAN OR A GIFT?

During this period of unrest and at least temporary instability, your 40s child may need a bit of financial help. Loaning money to kids can be awkward and grounds for dissension. Some families are successful in writing out contracts with scheduled repayment dates. However, most families, including ourselves, have trouble with this kind of formal planning. Working out such details about money given to kids is uncomfortable and can be a source of tension. After hearing all sorts of stories we have come to the conclusion that if you really are worried about being repaid, don't make a loan in the first place. The expectation of being repaid runs the risk of becoming a nagging concern for both of you. And as always, our feeling is that anything that is hurtful or disturbs family relationships should be avoided at all costs.

If you can afford it, just give the money without expectations of being repaid. Accept the reality that in some form or another parents are always on the giving end. Someday your kids will be in the same role with their kids. Parents give and kids accept. Didn't someone once say, "Joy is in the giving, *not* the receiving"?

"IT'S A WHOLE NEW WORLD!"

"You bet it is," said one parent. "Sometimes I feel almost prehistoric. My grandson asked me what television programs I watched when I was his age. His mouth dropped open when I told him television didn't exist when I was a child."

"What did you do for fun?" was his astonished reaction.

Generation gaps—everyone has encountered them in one form or another. For today's parents of 40- to 49-year-olds and beyond, the chasm between them and their kids in some ways is enormous. Lifestyles in the twenty-first century are dramatically different from anything they ever knew.

Let's for a moment consider marriage and having kids. The familiar childhood jingle, "First comes love, then comes marriage, then comes baby in a baby carriage," pretty much summed up the expected pattern in the past. However, today marriage and having a baby may be totally unrelated, as one parent of a 43-year-old discovered.

His single 43-year-old daughter had no intentions of marrying. "She's had lots of opportunities. She threw them all over. She didn't want a husband. As she told us, too many of her friends married and got divorced after the kids were born. She felt that getting married was an unnecessary step. What she did want was a baby, not a husband.

"We've known for some time how much she wanted a baby. She never made a secret of her desire. What she never told us was how she was going about it. My wife found out when our daughter was five months pregnant. I didn't know until later. Artificial insemination. She didn't even know the donor's name.

"My wife and I were with her the night the baby was born. A beautiful little baby girl. Yes, I felt strange. There should have been a father. When my daughter was born, I was waiting outside the delivery room. The nurse didn't know our daughter wasn't married. She had come on duty that evening.

"'Shall I get the father?' she asked my daughter.

"'There is no father—well, no one I know personally,' was

her answer. The doctor laughed appreciatively. He had been most supportive of our daughter during the pregnancy. I won't forget that dawn. I went to the window of her room and looked out. I wanted to cry. Yes, I admit it I wanted to cry my heart out. I never let her know how I felt.

"She came home to us for about a week and has been on her own since then. I surprised myself. I never thought I would get used to the idea. That has passed. I only have to look at my daughter and see her happiness to remind myself, 'Who am I to judge?'

"I realize what had bugged me most. Telling people we knew, friends, having the rest of the world pass judgment. All that means nothing to me anymore. It was her decision. It's her life and her happiness."

A whole new world out there. Unmarried women having babies, singles living together with no intention of getting married, couples of the same sex marrying, marriages between individuals from different religions, ethnicities, and racial backgrounds are much more common than they ever were.

"It was so comfortable in the past," said one mother of a 54-year-old getting ready for a second divorce. "People married and stayed married. What has ever happened to the part of the marriage ceremony—'until death do us part'? Maybe it should be rewritten to something like 'marriage until the divorce and the next marriage.'"

There are any number of confounding situations parents of twenty-first-century 40s kids have to face. "My daughter has three kids. Her new husband has three. She's now expecting a baby. She's told the kids of her new husband to call me 'Granny.' I'm not so sure I feel comfortable. But then what do they call me? Step-Granny?"

What do parents do? How do you handle these situations? It's not always so easy to give up certain of your principles, your beliefs, and to compromise your values. After all, by the time you have kids in their 40s, you're older, and chances are, like so many older people, perhaps you're a little more conservative than you may have been in your youth.

One parent who was having trouble with the lifestyle of his son had to be reminded by friends that, at the same age, he had been quite radical. He grew out of that stage and now voted Republican and wore suits, starched shirts, and ties to work.

It is not our place or the right of anyone to advise parents to throw over cherished beliefs, but we do suggest parents consider the alternatives. First of all, can they do anything about the choices their kids have made? We sincerely doubt it. No amount of lecturing will make the adult child change his or her mind about a particular lifestyle they have chosen. If that style is in no way harmful to the child or to anyone else, it's probably wisest to step back.

Above all, you do not want to alienate yourself from your child. It's not very much fun to get older as a parent without the support, interest, and concern of your child. Recognizing there are some choices in life your kids will make that you can do nothing about and then moving forward will be the best thing you can do for yourself and for your adult son or daughter.

The new third wife may not be your choice. You aren't living with her. Your son is. Your daughter is divorcing one husband and marrying another with kids of his own. It's her happiness that counts. And the grandkids, well, if being called Granny makes you unhappy, come up with another name you and the new stepgrandchildren choose.

Behaving in a compromising way is only tough at the moment you give in. From then on it's easy sailing. It's not going to be difficult, because don't forget, by the time you have kids this old, 40 to 50-plus, you appreciate the importance of filling "the unforgiving minute with sixty seconds' worth of distance run." Not one precious second deserves to be wasted on bitterness, rancor, or hatred.

THE CHANGING PARENT-CHILD RELATIONSHIP

Up to this point, we've looked at the parent-child relationship through a psychological lens that emphasizes the adult children's needs, the adult children's concerns, and the adult children's problems. It clearly is a child-centered point of view. In discussing the role of the parent, we have underscored the importance of empathic understanding, patience, tolerance, and generosity, sometimes at the expense of the parent's immediate needs and desires.

At this stage, however, there are changes in the wind. Your kids have grown older, and so have you. As a parent of 40s kids, there is a shift in the relationship between you and your children. No longer is it reasonable to focus exclusively on the needs and concerns of your children; your own needs and your own concerns at this stage of life must be recognized and taken into account.

After all those years of fulfilling family obligations and responsibilities, you've earned certain *parental rights* in relation to your kids. We urge you to exercise these rights, but don't overdo them. Think of yourself still as the parent. Someday they will be the age you are now, and they will remember and thank you for having served as a model for how they might behave with their children.

THE RIGHT TO REMINISCE

"I sat in the center of the bomber. It was World War II. The radar screen was in front of me and the blips were blipping all over the screen. They were planes moving. That was my job, following the blips. And the pilots scared the s___ out of us. They had no fear and. . . ."

When kids are in their 20s and the story is being told, a cell phone hopefully chimes, fingers drum on an armrest; the body language of 20- to 29-year-olds is pretty clear. Escape is on the kids' minds. In the 30s they stay put, perhaps even hear the story out, but they could not for the life of them repeat one word. They may not even recognize when the reminiscence has ended. Thirties are totally absorbed in the demands of their family and careers. They have selective hearing.

How wonderful for parents when kids enter their 40s and beyond. Each passing year of the next decades becomes more satisfying and rewarding for parents. Kids of this age listen, not always with the concentrated attention you might desire, but they do hear you out. In fact, they may even go so far as to silence a grandchild who interrupts a monologue.

When you have kids 40 and up, you've *earned* the right to reminisce. We don't for a moment think you should go overboard in exercising this privilege. Rather, proceed with caution. Drop a reference to your past into the conversation. Elaborate on the event. If you enjoy retelling a story you've told before, by all means relate the anecdote. We're certain you can add some embellishments to keep everyone's interest even if the kids correct you. "Mom, you exaggerate. We did not big game hunt when we were living in Uganda that summer. We did see big game, but we were in a car."

Kids 40 and beyond, particularly the older 40s and into the 50s, are amazingly patient. There's nothing wrong with your taking advantage of this patience as long as you remember to exercise some restraint. Perhaps you will be recounting the reminiscences to a new audience—grandchildren. If you catch grandchildren at the right moment, they will be entranced with past adventures in your life.

You may even be an assignment. Suddenly American public schools have become history oriented and third and fourth graders are interviewing grandparents about their childhoods. In all seriousness, there is an age when kids are curious about their origins as long as it doesn't take too long to tell and get in the way of a play date.

One grandmother has begun her autobiography. "I want the kids to know who I was and where they came from. They may not care now. Someday they will be interested. I'm up to page fifty-six and I haven't even reached my teens!" She plans the autobiography in a number of volumes.

Wanting to know where we came from is something we all feel. We have profound regrets that whole blank spaces of our heritage are unknown. We know our pasts go a lot further back than about 1895 at Ellis Island, but we can't search them out because we have no clues.

So reminiscing is fine. T. S. Eliot wrote, "Time present and time past is contained in time future." Parents can and should be the link to the family's past. However, when eyes glaze, the TV volume is turned up a few more decibels, and kids suddenly remember pressing obligations, parents should recognize and heed the signs. Save your stories for another day when you once again have a captive audience.

THE RIGHT TO BE DEPENDENT

No other phone call means as much to us as the one that begins, "Hi. It's me. A quick call. . . ." One or the other son has taken a moment to make a phone call. We're not shy about reporting the pleasure we feel. A few words are enough to set the tone of our day.

We're also not reluctant to tell you that we expectantly wait for a son's invitation to come over on a weekend night. We cherish the couple of hours when the family has dinner together—a barbecue, the old staples of Chinese takeout or pizzas. On the way home in the car without any embarrassment we admit to each other that we really look forward to those moments. The length of time doesn't matter. In fact, after a couple of hours, all of us have had enough. We're ready to go our separate ways, to return to our own pursuits, knowing that the following week we will meet again.

After all those years of doing and giving as much as you could to your kids, it's certainly all right, we feel, for parents to recognize their dependencies. Parents, including ourselves, have long been accustomed to being on the giving end. It takes a little adjusting to realize that with the passage of time how much we want and need the phone call, the several hours together—to accept without apologies to ourselves any strong feelings of dependency.

In our studies we discovered that one problem parents of 40- to 49-year-olds had was their own discomfort with feelings of dependence with their kids. Men, in particular, had a tough time.

"I'll do anything to avoid asking my son for help. Sure he knows more than I do about a lot of things. But it makes me uncomfortable to ask him. I'm the one used to being asked. He had to come to me. He's asked me, 'Dad, let me help you. I know a helluva lot more about finance than you do. You'll go to someone else—why not your own son?' He's right. A stranger would be easier. The idea of my having to ask my son about the stock market doesn't make sense. I guess I still see him as a little kid."

Dads are used to being in charge. Undoubtedly their reactions have something to do with macho feelings. Fathers should be able to manage their own affairs, stand on their own two feet, not turn to their kids for advice. Wimps do that. However, once dads get over that irrational reluctance and recognize there's nothing wrong with being dependent when the occasion arises, they certainly can feel more relaxed. They may discover a son's investment advice will pay off.

For many mothers, including myself, turning to kids for assistance also takes some adjusting. In my case I was accustomed to helping my sons in different situations when they were young. Being put in a dependent position at my age makes me very uncomfortable. My experience with the computer world was traumatic.

Having grown up with a mechanical typewriter, moving on to an electric typewriter was a major step. This was nothing compared to learning how to handle a computer. It was my sons' idea I get one. They assured me writing would be a lot easier, to say nothing of the joys of the Internet and e-mail. I had problems. I had to call them for help. I suffered through every call.

One time I called California in desperation, practically in tears, because a manuscript had disappeared into computer space. I will not tell you the kids were always gracious. They did try, though after endlessly repeating instructions, their level of tolerance was sorely tested. To sum it all up, the experience of dependency was not the greatest.

But now that they are both beyond 40-plus, I no longer am troubled. In fact, just recently a desperate call about a lost file didn't phase me in the slightest. A son responded with complete patience. That's the right of a parent of 40-plus kids. Kids of this age, you will discover, rise to the occasion. In addition to your getting needed help, your kids benefit. Think of it as fun for them to have the tables turned. Parents no longer call all the shots, hand out advice. Instead they're the ones who have to do the asking. The files, incidentally, were popped back into place and backup disks made.

THE RIGHT TO BE INDEPENDENT

One important right parents have earned is their right to be independent. Kids sometimes forget this. It's understandable. They think about your aging. They may watch like hawks for signs of decline. A little misstep like the forgetting of a name or date might make them furrow their brows in concern.

In a sense they are only doing what you have done over the years. Turnabout is fair play, or is it? The invasion of your personal space might be a bit troublesome. You'll have to tell your kids to hold back. You have to remind them you're still the parent and they are your kids. However, before you get all uptight about their intrusions, it might be helpful for you to check out what they are worrying about. Once their concerns are clear to you, you can ease their worrying and stem the tide of questioning.

For example, one widower in his mid-70s has a delightful new girlfriend. She started out as a housekeeper in his home after his wife died and gradually moved up in status. Not too long ago she moved in with him, and the relationship progressed.

They currently share a bedroom, a fact which astonished the 40s kids and caused a great deal of raised eyebrows with the college-age grandchildren. "Grandpa having an affair" was commented upon with surprise by one grandson who had lived with a different woman each year of his four years at college.

"I never asked you about your living arrangements," Grandpa told the grandson. "What I do is my business."

Although the kids were not all that happy, they didn't overtly react until they heard about wedding plans. "How could you marry her? I understand living with the woman, but marriage," said one daughter who had played the romantic field to the hilt when she was young. "What will people say? You can't get married again at your age!"

The dialogue back and forth went on for some time until the father finally gained some insight into the problem.

"It occurred to me that the kids worried about their inheritances. I told them I was going to marry this woman. She would benefit from my pension and social security. But I assured them she would not inherit any money from my investments and savings.

"I showed the kids my will, gave them the name of the lawyer who held all the documents. I had to laugh. Magically all their objections vanished. My son asked to be my best man. My daughter is going to be a matron of honor. My new wife hasn't any family. Once the kids were reassured they weren't going to lose anything by the marriage, their objections faded away."

If parents have funds or possessions, kids, especially the late 40s and 50-plusses, worry about their inheritances. Will a sibling get more, and if so, why? How is the estate going to be divided? Of course, there can be concerns about money at any age. However, the concerns often realistically surface when kids have older parents. It doesn't hurt for you to clarify matters. Everyone will relax a little knowing that whatever is left they will get a fair share. And it's probably just as wise to let them know if nothing is going to be left. This way they won't be in the position of building up unrealistic fantasies about what splurges in lifestyle they might make after you depart. Make sure they know the value of what you have. There can be a lot of myths of the value of your possessions. *Antiques Roadshow*, otherwise delightful, unfortunately has contributed to generation dissension.

After viewing one program, a mid-40s woman frantically called her father. "Where is that little china figure you had above the fireplace mantle?"

"I threw it out."

"How could you?"

"It was worthless."

"Dad. You threw away a fortune. My inheritance," she inadvertently blurted out. "I saw a piece exactly like that on the *Antiques Roadshow*. Do you have any idea what it was worth? Please check the garbage."

"I told you it fell off the mantle and broke."

"Dad, it could have been repaired. That was a seventeenth-century porcelain figure of a midget with a fishing rod. It was just like the one I saw on the show."

"No way," said the father. "The one we had was a plaster-of-Paris dwarf, one of the seven—Dopey. It was hollow."

Dead silence. "Are you sure, Dad?"

"Of course I'm sure. We got it at a street carnival. Tommy (a grandchild) won it when he threw a ball and hit a duck."

The moral of this story told to us by one parent is to make sure your kids know what you have and what everything is worth. Everyone, including yourself, will be a lot happier. Far better to know it is a plaster-of-Paris dwarf while the father is still living than for the daughter to unrealistically plan her inheritance perhaps years down the road.

THE RIGHT TO BE YOURSELF

One of the most intriguing features of aging is that, as we grow older, we become more our true selves. That is, as the external demands of jobs, family responsibilities, and social as well as community obligations decrease, our own needs, our own natural inclinations come more to the forefront of our personalities. Accept this time as your opportunity to relax, let down some of your guards. You can wear a Yankees baseball jacket over a sunflowered sleeveless dress because there's a chill on a summer evening and not be met with open-mouthed astonishment.

This tendency to become more our true selves might cause embarrassment to your kids. We faced this problem in our own lives. After three-plus decades of being a professor wearing jackets, starched shirts, ties, and pressed pants, Joel decided he would wear only casual clothing. Think gym-type sweatpants and loose shirts. Determined to be totally self-sufficient, he insisted on doing his own tailoring. Now this presented a problem. He could not always judge the length and measure the hem. The result of his efforts has consistently been *too* short pants. This in itself would not have been noticed if the pants and socks were the same color. However, the sweatpants are typically black, and he favors white athletic socks and sneakers.

Our impeccably dressed kids and their wives have been amazingly tolerant. We assure you the costume has *not* gone unnoticed and has been remarked on innumerable times with no effect. They just gave up—well, almost. An important family affair was to take place. Everyone tried to tactfully get Joel to change his customary attire. Frankly, no progress was made. Whispered campaigns had no effect. We assure you it was an agonizing period.

Joel's feeling was "So be it. I've learned to live with everyone else's idiosyncrasies. They can live with mine." He was holding his ground. And then, when the date for the event was perilously near, he relented. There was palpable shock when Joel appeared in the traditional blue jacket, gold buttons, gray flannel pants, tie, and starched shirt. *The moral of the story is always be true to yourself, up to a point.*

THE ACTIVE FIFTIES AND BEYOND
Parenting the 50-Plus

The American culture has prolonged education. Less than a century ago, an elementary school diploma was considered sufficient to prepare people for productive lives. Gradually parents and educators have tacked on the need for more and more schooling: middle school, high school, college, graduate school, professional training of one sort or another. There doesn't seem to be an end point when we sit back comfortably and say, "Enough learning. Can we possibly learn more?"

Our unqualified answer is a resounding "Yes." The never-ending concept of education is particularly appropriate for parenting. It is a fallacy to assume that by the time you have a 50-plus child you have learned enough to react appropriately no matter the circumstances. First of all, as we have indicated a number of times, parenting is forever. You can never abdicate or grow out of the role. There are always new lessons to master.

Although knowledge you acquired parenting 0- to 49-year-old children provides a good foundation, there is a significant difference in the skills you're going to need to successfully parent 50-plus kids. There is a sound basis for this difference.

Although you have certainly changed during the course of the 49 years of parenting that lie behind you, the changes in parents when kids are 50-plus are dramatic. First of all, at this time in your life, you start to become more and more yourself. By this we mean you start to shed a lot of superficialities such as styles of behaving, and controls. You may, without intentional awareness, forget some of our useful instruction that governed your behavior in the past decades.

You enter an age we will call "natural." This simply means that as parents of a 50-plus, you begin to lose a lot of inhibitions. Your feelings are more up-front. You forget about diplomacy or repression. As you start to cut loose, we urge you not to forget that you still are parents. Your kids may be 50, 55, 60, 65-plus, but you still are Mom or Dad no matter what. The kids are still sensitive. Don't lose sight of this fact.

However, on the plus side, if you transgress, you tend not to worry as much about your behavior, with one exception—a daughter-in-law or a son-in-law. Therefore, although it may be a bit of a struggle, do try and retain as much as you can of the knowledge you've gained by the time you reach this point. We have great faith in your ability to rise to the challenge.

CHARACTERISTICS OF 50-PLUS KIDS

Hopefully vigorous, sexually active, energized by their careers, 50-plus kids think of themselves as more interesting, infinitely more exciting than they were as teenagers. In fact, for some, the age may be thought of as "teenage revisited." They buy snorkeling equipment and bigger and faster cars, forgetting that at 65 their reflexes aren't the greatest and they are, according to statistics, more accident-prone. They may plan unusual trips that test them physically.

They aren't totally cavalier in their behavior. They do think of money, planning for the future. They economize, for example, buying less expensive bottles of wine for guests that don't count. Regardless of their income, they do make sure they get senior discounts at theaters, museums, on trains, and airlines. For the most part, bills are paid promptly. Fifty-plus kids do not like to build up high credit card balances. The practice can be very disquieting.

If they like to travel, they will join groups and go sightseeing, distinctly visible marching around Williamsburg wearing colorful pantsuits and hats. On vacations they make it a point to get up early for ranger-led nature hikes, making sure everyone within earshot hears them say, "Not too bad for an old guy like me to get up early, to take a ten mile walk."

The age can be flirtatious. Dressing nattily, the men make charming remarks to younger women. If widowed, they may seriously pursue older women. As the years go on, the 50-plus women often pay more attention to their hair and makeup. They may have standing Friday afternoon beauty shop appointments to get hair and nails done. In the 40 to 49 stage, and even in the earlier decades, their children indulged in such luxuries. Mother had little or no time for frivolous activities. Life was far too busy.

A lot of changes are taking place. Thoughts about retirement, where to live, social security, and income from other investment plans characterize a great deal of their leisure thinking. The age group struggles with such questions as whether to move to that condo, downsize our home, go to Florida, or stay in the same area. Those with active careers think about when they should call a halt, give up positions they worked so hard to attain. It is a big mistake to assume that your 50-plus kids are static. They're alive and active, on the go, even if there are a few more aches and pains and the number of pills that must be taken has significantly increased.

YOUR ROLE AS A PARENT OF KIDS 50-PLUS

Unfortunately for you, the renewed vigor that envelops your 50-plus kids may spill over and threaten the nice balance of your life. For example, you may be persuaded to come and visit them at the summer house they rented for two weeks. Without thinking, you make the tragic mistake of going. When you initially showed reluctance to join the family, your 50-plus kid whispered about how Mom and Dad have lost all their get up and go. The real truth was you no longer can stand insect-ridden campgrounds, nor do your "older" feet relish a pebble- and shell-covered sandy beach.

You're going to have to be patient with your 50-plus kids. Draw a line about what you will or won't do. For example, your 50-plus kids may read some study done by a young gerontology student demonstrating that people are happier and live longer if they have pets. It's nice this researcher received a doctorate for the study, but if your children offer you bird, cat, goldfish, or miniature schnauzer and you do not want a pet, give a firm "No."

However, remember before you complain too much or reject too many of the offers, just be thankful and appreciative your kids of 50-plus are still talking to you. Enjoy the pleasant shock of receiving more phone calls and impromptu visits than you ever have before except, of course, when they were in college and needed extra money.

It's fun to hear from them and see them much more often. Deep down you're delighted they have reached the age when their lives are changing, winding down, and less frenetic. This means they now have unspent energy and increased time which you hope they will devote to paying attention to you. How marvelous they are willing to listen a little more, something they didn't do when they were in that rebellious 40- to 49-year-old stage or in the self-preoccupied 30s decade. We certainly know the 20s egocentrics would not have paid attention in the least.

All in all, it's really quite nice to have 50-plus kids. We urge you, just in case you are somewhat wary, to enjoy every minute of the age. Accept the fact that you will make some bumbling mistakes. What will be gratifying is the kids won't get uptight or angry when they show up in a big lumbering sports vehicle and you blurt out, "Why in the world did you buy such a ridiculous monstrosity masquerading as a car?" Instead of reacting with anger, they smile. Privately they will attribute your foolish lapses of decorum to the onset of Alzheimer's.

When you meet your kids' friends, they won't bat an eyelash when you tell these friends that, "I know you people. My kids told me about your dreadfully expensive house that was terribly overpriced!"

No one, including grandchildren, who can be more judgmental of your behavior than your own kids, will say anything critical when a box of candy is passed around and they watch you turn over every piece to see which has a pink crème center with a walnut, your favorite.

FACING YOUR OWN AGING

In some cultures there are built-in systems for coping with the aged. The old people may simply move in with their children. In Japan at one period, old people packed their belongings in a little knapsack and climbed a mountain to die. There is a famous story of the guilt-ridden son who followed his mother's trail and carried her back to his home.

The American culture frowns on and discourages multi-generational living. "The last thing I want to do is to have to live with my kids." We couldn't possibly count the number of times this was said to us during the course of our interviewing. If that concept is as frightening to you as it is to us, make sure you have alternative plans ready to put into operation for such a time as that might be an unwilling event in your life.

Far too many books are being written about how to manipulate older people, from estate planning to where they are going to live and the nursing home they will enter. We believe all these things should be your decisions to make. Don't wait until you aren't capable of making plans. The only way you can prevent this from happening is to make all the decisions about your future *before* you are unable. Don't ever relinquish this prerogative to be captain of your fate and master of your soul. You will be hopping mad and bitter if you do. A parent is a parent forever; don't give up that right and privilege. Hang on tenaciously to your rights while you have rational faculties.

The pleasure of parenting older children is by no means only egocentric. We've felt it important to note a few of the plusses simply because by the time you have kids this age and have been through what you've been through, you more than deserve rewards. However, a strong word of warning. Your role as parents is far from finished. Up until now you've given your kids a lot. You've perhaps helped them out financially. Your services with their kids, your grandchildren, have been useful. Everything you've done has been important—not necessarily earthshaking, but useful.

At this point, however, you are going to be able to give them one of the most valuable and important gifts ever—a gift they will treasure and one they can pass down to the next generation when it is their turn to be in your position.

THE GIFT YOU CAN GIVE TO YOUR AGING KIDS

Throughout this book one theme has remained central: A parent is a parent forever no matter the age of the kids. Although many of the suggestions we have made up until now have been tangible, whether it is never imposing on your kids by showing up at unexpected times, or helping out financially if you can when the going gets rough, at this time in life the greatest gift you can give to your kids will be your *attitude toward life.*

Over the years you've served as role model for your kids even though they may not have been aware that your behavior had any impact on their thinking. It is different now. The kids are older and undoubtedly more mature. What you do and how you behave will be noted and appreciated.

Your 50, 60, and 65-plus kids are concerned about their own aging. Your positive spirit, an acceptance of the reality of your growing older without letting age take away any of the excitement of living, will work wonders for your kids' psyches. You may not be able to best them in a tennis game, shoot under par and take home the trophy, or stay awake for the super late-night film, and your shape leaves a little to be desired, but they will see they have miles to run to catch up with your spirit and zest for life.

They will be thankful for not equating visits with Mom and Dad with concerns about having to sit through a litany of complaints, demands, or loneliness. Of course you won't always feel upbeat, but you can do your best to find other shoulders on which to rest your woes, which we sincerely hope are few and far between.

Thus, as we draw near to an end of our review of parenting it's super to end on an up note. You have an important role in kids' lives from the start to their senior citizen stage. It is possible that the joys of being parents of 50-plus kids really can surpass all the previous decades. However, our best suggestion, of course, is to enjoy and treasure them all!

A FINAL NOTE

Do children ever grow up? For that matter, do parents ever learn? This book was finished. We were unwinding. It was one son's forty-seventh birthday. He has a beautiful saltwater fish tank, his pride and joy. What could be a better gift than an incredibly expensive saltwater fish? When he was a child we bought goldfish. They are passé.

The fish store salesman suggested we purchase what he insisted was a magnificent fish. An experienced grandson took charge of putting the fish in the tank. It swam feebly around and then become motionless in a vertical position. I called the fish store. "I do not think you sold me a healthy fish."

"The fish needs to adjust. It's in shock."

The next several days I drove to my son's house to check on the fish's adjustment. On the third day there was no sign of the fish. Evidently, the fish had died, providing a grand feast for the survivors. Irate, I called the fish store to report the death and requested credit. The fish had been guaranteed.

Of course I was grilled on how the fish went into the tank. What had it been fed? Now it was a time to flaunt my age. "I was not born yesterday. Our grandson who knows about fish did everything correctly. That fish was sick." Reluctantly, they agreed to give my son credit.

Hurrying home I sat down at the computer and typed an e-mail to my son at his office. "Mickey (I'm the only one who calls him by a childhood nickname instead of a mature Michael), please go directly to the fish store on your way home. Do not forget. The store will credit you. You buy fish there regularly. Why didn't you tell me the fish died yesterday? By the way, Mickey, please don't forget to call your brother tomorrow. It's his birthday."

I was clearly upset about the expensive fish and the birthday call he might forget. His brother lives some distance away. After one sends an e-mail, there is no way to retrieve the message. Horror-struck, I realized what I had done. I had ordered a busy 47-year-old professional man to make a side trip home from work to a fish store and also to make a telephone call.

Joel was not consoling. In so many words he intimated, How stupid could I have been? I waited for an irate telephone call. I would deserve whatever our son had to say about a nagging mother treating him as if he were a twelve-year-old. I shuddered to think if that e-mail had been read by his secretary. Why did I send it to his office instead of to the house? More important, why did I send it anyway?

I suffered. I deserved whatever he had to say about my behavior. I decided not be defensive but to listen. I would then offer my abject apologies. I was practically in tears with worry. Just before dinner I once again checked the computer. A message!

"Mom, will go to fish store and get a new fish. Will call Jeff. Promise.

"Love Mickey."

Tears of relief! He wasn't angry! He wasn't even annoyed! And then I felt a warm glow. Kids do grow up. Parents? Well, about that we're not so sure.